Secrets of Sleep

SECRETS

OF

SLEEP

Alexander Borbély

Translated by Deborah Schneider

Basic Books, Inc., Publishers

NEW YORK

Library of Congress Cataloging-in-Publication Data

Borbély, Alexander A.
   Secrets of Sleep.

   Translation of: Das Geheimnis des Schlafs.
   Bibliography: p. 213
   Includes index.
   1. Sleep—Physiological aspects.   I. Title.
   QP425.B6713   1986   612'.821   85-73887
   ISBN   0-465-07592-4

Contents

Preface to the American Edition

It is a great pleasure for me to see my book appear in its English translation in the present American edition. Scientists in North America have made important contributions to sleep research, and public interest in this discipline has been always particularly great on the American continent. Nevertheless, sleep science is a truly international endeavor which is being pursued ever more vigorously throughout the world. I hope that this book will not only provide an easily readable account of recent developments, but that it will also convey some of the fascination and excitement that emanate from sleep and its numerous secrets. I thank Mr. Martin Kessler and his colleagues at Basic Books for their pleasant collaboration in preparing this volume.

—ALEXANDER BORBÉLY
Zurich, August 1986

Preface

When I give lectures on sleep, I am frequently asked by members of the audience to recommend a nontechnical book on sleep research. Unfortunately the literature on this subject is somewhat limited. Much good work has been done on special topics in the field, but no recent book offering a general survey of sleep research for the nonspecialist has been available. This is particularly regrettable in view of the fact that new and promising developments have taken place over the last few years. As the connection between sleep and biological rhythms has emerged more clearly, for example, our understanding of the regulation of sleep has increased significantly. The search for endogenous substances (that is, natural substances produced by the body itself) that promote sleep is a further example of an area of research in which great strides have been made in recent years. It was not only the existence of such new developments that motivated me to write this book, however, but also my own research work and the general fascination inherent in the subject as a whole. It has been my goal to provide an intelligible and lively account of important aspects of modern sleep research for the interested general reader. I hope that those readers who would like to delve more deeply into any of the topics can find useful information in the suggestions for further reading in the bibliography.

Sleep researchers need expensive equipment and laboratories for their experiments. My own research, on which I report in this book, has for many years received generous support both from the Institute of Pharmacology of the University of Zurich Medical School and from the Swiss National Foundation for the

Promotion of Scientific Research. I would here like to express my gratitude to both institutions. However, even with the best technical equipment one cannot pursue research on sleep all by oneself. I have had the good fortune to collaborate in Zurich with capable and hardworking colleagues and students; in particular I would like to thank Dr. Irene Tobler, my colleague of long standing, who contributed significantly to most of the projects undertaken in the last few years. The friendly cooperation of Professor Inge Strauch of the Department of Psychology and Professor Dietrich Lehmann of the Department of Neurology led to the foundation of our joint Laboratory for Experimental and Clinical Sleep Research as well as to joint projects and colloquia.

A considerable part of this book was written in the Swiss Alps, to which I retreated in order to be able to collect my thoughts free from outside distractions. I am grateful to my family for their understanding and support of this undertaking. My sister, Esther Borbély, who read the first draft, discovered numerous inconsistencies and made many stylistic improvements. Although she is still not entirely content with the final version, I would like to express my thanks for her great help. I am especially grateful to Dr. Hans Rössner for his criticism of the manuscript, his many suggestions, and his active support and assistance in the preparation of the book. Dr. Irene Tobler offered valuable suggestions on several chapters and helped with the illustrations. Finally, I would like to thank Karin Schwarz for the illustrations and Beatrice Pfeifer for typing the manuscript.

—ALEXANDER BORBÉLY
Zurich, January 1984

Secrets of Sleep

1

A Historical View of Sleep

The world, it seems, does not possess even those of us who
are adults completely, but only up to two thirds; one third
of us is still quite unborn. Every time we wake in the
morning it is like a new birth.

—SIGMUND FREUD
Introductory Lectures on Psycho-Analysis

When we go to bed at night, we enter an altered state of consciousness that lasts for a number of hours. We cease to see,
hear, and feel consciously what occurs around us. The world of
sleep and the world of wakefulness are so different that each
of us could be said to live in two worlds. The difference appears
particularly striking when we wake up suddenly during the
night and are not immediately aware of where we are. The
French writer Marcel Proust has given a beautiful description
of this transitional state:

> But for me it was enough if, in my own bed, my sleep was
> so heavy as completely to relax my consciousness; for then
> I lost all sense of the place in which I had gone to sleep, and
> when I awoke at midnight, not knowing where I was, I could
> not be sure at first of who I was; I had only the most rudimen-
> tary sense of existence, such as may lurk and flicker in the

depths of an animal's consciousness; I was more destitute of human qualities than the cave-dweller; but then the memory, not yet of the place in which I was, but of various other places where I had lived, and might now very possibly be, would come like a rope let down from heaven to draw me up out of the abyss of not-being, from which I could never have escaped by myself: in a flash I would traverse and surmount centuries of civilisation, and out of a half-visualised succession of oil-lamps, followed by shirts with turned-down collars, would put together by degrees the component parts of my ego.[1]

Many people take sleep so much for granted that they hardly ever stop to reflect on its origin and meaning. Only when it is disturbed does sleep become a subject of conscious thought and a "problem." The purpose of this book is to show that sleep, as one of the basic processes of life, has become an increasingly interesting subject of study for scientists in recent years. The results of new research suggest that answers may be found to questions that have occupied mankind for centuries. I have also tried to give an impression of how many different scientific disciplines make contributions to the field of research on sleep. Virtually no other area of modern science combines a comparable importance for basic research with such a direct bearing on our everyday life, and as a branch of science it is also unique because long years of experience make every one of us, so to speak, a specialist in the field.

On the Word *Sleep*

The English word *sleep* is of Germanic origin and derives from the Gothic word *sleps,* through the Old and Middle High German *slaf.* The modern German word *Schlaf* and the Dutch *slaap* share the same derivation. The German word *schlafen* (to sleep) originally meant *schlapp werden* (to grow tired or slack) and is related to the adjective *schlapp* (slack, weak, limp). In what follows we shall see that in modern sleep research the increasing slackness of the muscles, or the reduction of muscle tension, serves as an important indicator of different stages of sleep.

The word *slumber* also has a Germanic origin and an Indo-Germanic root, *slu* (slack, drooping). The German equivalent, *schlummern,* first appeared in Low and Middle High German and was introduced into the written language in the sixteenth century by Martin Luther. The word *doze* has a Germanic origin as well, cognate with the modern German word of the same meaning, *dösen. Dizzy* (German *duselig*) has the same root, as does the German word *dunstig* (hazy, misty). *Dozing* can thus also describe a mentally hazy state. The words *drowsy* and *drowse* are of uncertain origin, but they probably derive from the Old English *drusian* (to sink, become slow) and *dreosan* (to fall).

The basic term *sleep* has led to the coining of certain expressions that have little to do with sleep itself in a direct sense. Thus *to fall asleep* is sometimes used as a euphemism for *to die,* while *the sleep that knows not breaking* means death. *To sleep on something* means to delay a decision until the next day, in order to put a certain problem into perspective. *To sleep together* or *to sleep with someone* refers to an act that is not directly connected with the phenomenon of sleep itself; just as in the case of death the use of a euphemism or a less direct term is often preferred.

Some English words pertaining to sleep derive from the Latin word for sleep, *somnus,* such as *somnolent* and *somnambulist* (sleep-walker). A somniloquist is a person who talks in his sleep. The Latin word for a deep sleep, *sopor,* was also the name of the Roman god of sleep; from this root we derive the English word *soporific* (making sleepy, causing sleep). The name of the Greek god of sleep, Hypnos, is contained in the words *hypnosis* (a putting to sleep) and *hypnotic* (sleep-promoting). Most Indo-Germanic and Romance languages contain the root *som* or *son* cognate to the Latin *somnus* in their word for sleep: French *sommeil;* Italian *sonno;* Spanish *sueño;* Portuguese *sono;* Romanian *somn;* Swedish *sömn;* Danish *sovn;* Russian *son;* Polish *sen;* Bulgarian *sun;* Serbo-Croatian *san;* Czech *spanek;* and Hindi *sona.*

In other languages sleep is called *hypnos* (Greek); *alvás* (Hungarian); *uni* (Finnish); *uyku* (Turkish); *shenah* (Hebrew); *nemuri* (Japanese); *shui jiao* (Chinese); *nidura* (Telugu, a South Indian language); and *lala* (Zulu).

Sleep—The Brother of Death

The myths of ancient Greece portray both gentle sleep, Hypnos, and pitiless death, Thanatos, as sons of the goddess of night, Nyx. The Roman poet Ovid called sleep a "counterfeit of death." "He lives in a cave on the banks of the river Lethe, where the sun never penetrates. Poppies and countless herbs bloom before the cavern's entrance, from which night distills the juices of sleep to moisten the earth." For the early Germanic tribes sleep and death were also brothers, and both were called the sandman. According to Kuhlen, a specialist in the history of sleep remedies, this word derives from the verb *to send* and means a messenger who is sent, but it also describes the feeling of tired children ("It feels like sand in my eyes").[2] The stillness of a sleeping person has something uncanny about it. When we are asleep, we are exposed to the dangers of the world. Will we awake again from this mysterious state? In the face of this worrying question it is not surprising that people say a prayer before going to sleep and, for example, recommend their souls to the care of guardian angels. "I lie down and sleep; I wake again, for the Lord sustains me," says the Third Psalm. The believer can sleep peacefully and without fear, knowing that the Lord is keeping watch. "Behold, he who keeps Israel will neither slumber nor sleep. The Lord is your keeper" (Psalm 121:4–5). The Book of Genesis mentions sleep in the account of the Creation. No ordinary sleep is meant, but an unusually deep sleep (*tardema* in Hebrew), into which God causes Adam to fall in order to remove one of his ribs for the creation of Eve.

Peaceful sleep can at first glance easily be confused with death, however. Thus sleep as seeming death is also a frequent motif in sagas, poetry, and fairy tales. In Shakespeare's play, Juliet takes a drug to induce a deathlike sleep for several days and so to escape the unwelcome care of her family. Unfortunately not only the family is fooled but also her suitor Romeo, and so the story ends tragically. Snow White has a better time of it, for although she appears to be lying dead in her coffin, at the decisive moment she wakes up again after all. The "record" for sleeping is no doubt held by Briar Rose, the "Sleeping Beauty." In this case it is not a drug but an otherwise harmless injury that puts her to sleep, as foretold, for a hundred years. She does not fall asleep by herself but has a great deal of company: the king, the queen, and the entire court, along with horses, dogs, pigeons, and flies. Plants are clearly unaffected by the spell, however, since a hedge of briars grows up, covering the entire palace. The prince's kiss coincides exactly with the end of the ordained hundred-year-long period of sleep; it only appears to be the cause of everyone's reawakening but is certainly the main cause of the happy ending.

We have dealt thus far with sleep as a state resembling death, but it is also possible to ask the same question in reverse: To what degree can death be regarded as a state similar to sleep? In the Gospel according to John there is a particularly striking passage on the illness of Lazarus, which takes up this question. Jesus says to his disciples, " 'Our friend Lazarus has fallen asleep, but I go to awaken him out of sleep.' The disciples said to him, 'Lord, if he has fallen asleep, he will recover. Now Jesus had spoken of his death, but they thought that he meant taking rest in sleep. Then Jesus told them plainly, 'Lazarus is dead.' "

Jesus goes with his disciples to the grave where the dead man has already been lying for four days, and calls with a loud voice, " 'Lazarus, come out.' The dead man came out, his hands and feet bound with bandages, and his face wrapped with a cloth." The dead man thus comes back to life as if from a deep sleep.

7

Above and beyond this biblical passage human beings have long been moved to ask whether death is truly the end of life, or whether it might be a sleeplike state from which there could be some possible awakening after all. However, the discussion of this problem, even though it concerns many people today, would lead us too far from our actual subject.

Sleep—A State of Blessedness or of Dull Ignorance?

In Eastern philosophies and religions sleep has sometimes been depicted as the real and true human state, in which the individual and the universe are at one. The Chinese philosopher Chuang-tzu (300 B.C.) wrote, "Everything is one; during sleep the soul, undistracted, is absorbed into this unity; when awake, distracted, it sees the different beings."[3]

According to the ancient Indian philosophical texts of the Upanishads, four states of being exist: (1) the waking state common to all men; (2) the dreaming state; (3) the deep-sleep state; (4) the fourth (superconscious) state, "the very Self." Deep sleep *(susupta)* is the state in which one desires nothing and dreams nothing. In another passage of the Upanishads deep sleep is brought into connection with the real self: "Now when one is thus sound asleep, composed, serene, and knows no dream, that is the Self (Ātman), that is the immortal, the fearless, that is Brahma."[4]

The Judeo-Christian tradition has rarely regarded sleep as a desirable or higher state. Thus we find in the Old Testament the warning "Love not sleep, lest you come to poverty; open your eyes, and you will have plenty of bread" (Proverbs 20:13). Only that sleep which has been well earned through hard work is good sleep: "Sweet is the sleep of a laborer, whether he eats little or much; but the surfeit of the rich will not let him sleep" (Ecclesiastes 5:12).

Sleep as a symbol of lassitude, dull ignorance, and lack of faith occurs in Socrates' speech in his own defense before the court of Athens, where he describes himself as a gadfly of the people:

> If you take my advice, you will spare me. But you, perhaps, might be angry, like people awakened from a nap, and might slap me, as Anytus advises, and easily kill me; then you would pass the rest of your lives in slumber, unless God, in his care for you, should send someone else to sting you.[5]

Awakening is often understood in Christianity in a metaphorical sense; in the New Testament, for example, we find the summons "Awake, O sleeper, and arise from the dead, and Christ shall give you light" (Ephesians 5:14). The following hymn by Thomas Ken (1637–1711) also issues a summons to awake and begin a new life:

> Awake, my soul, and with the sun
> Thy daily stage of duty run;
> Shake off dull sloth, and joyful rise
> To pay thy morning sacrifice.
> Redeem thy misspent moments past,
> And live this day as if thy last;
> Improve thy talent with due care;
> For the great day thyself prepare.[6]

Eastern cultures also use the idea of awakening from sleep in a similar metaphorical sense, as the name Buddha shows, for example: "the Enlightened One," "the Awakened One," whereby *Buddha* derives from *budh* (to awaken).

Early Attempts to Explain Sleep: From Philosophy to Science

Philosophers and physicians in ancient Greece attempted to explain the origins of sleep in writings that have come down to us.[7] Empedocles, creator of the doctrine of the four elements, according to which nothing is created or destroyed but only joined or disjoined out of the elements fire, air, water, and earth, believed that sleep follows from a slight cooling of the heat contained in the blood, that is to say, a separation of the element fire from the three others. Hippocrates, "the father of medicine," concluded from the cooling of the limbs of a sleeping person that sleep is caused by the retreat of blood and warmth into the inner regions of the body.

According to the great natural philosopher Aristotle, the immediate cause of sleep is to be sought in the food we eat, which he supposed gives off fumes into the veins. The heat of the body, he thought, then drives these fumes into the head, where they collect and cause sleepiness. They then cool off in the brain and sink back into the lower parts of the body, drawing heat away from the heart. This process leads finally to sleep, which lasts until food has been digested and the pure blood destined for the upper regions of the body distilled from the impure blood. Alexander of Aphrodisias, an interpreter of Aristotle's theories who lived in the second or third century A.D., developed the theory of heat further and argued that tiredness causes the body to dry out and thus lose heat; this leads in the end to sleep.

In the Middle Ages (twelfth century) Hildegard of Bingen, a German Benedictine nun, wrote mystical treatises on medicine and nature in which she emphasized the parallels between sleep and food, connecting both with the Fall of Adam. Kuhlen describes her rather singular views as follows:

Human beings consist of two parts: waking and sleeping. It thus follows that the human body is nourished in two ways, namely, by food and rest. Before the Fall, Adam's sleep was a "sleep of submersion" *(sopor)*, that is, a deep, contemplative sleep, and his food was food for the eyes alone; both sleep and food existed merely to delight and edify the soul and spirit. The Fall made his body weak and feeble, more like the body of a dead person than a living one. Since then human beings have needed strengthening through both nourishment and rest. Sleep has become a normal condition for all people. Just as food causes the flesh to grow, so the marrow *(medulla)*, which is thinned and weakened by the waking state, regenerates itself and grows again during sleep.[8]

In the sixteenth century the famous physician Paracelsus strove to relate medicine more closely to nature. He had very firm views on many subjects, sleep among them; he was of the opinion that natural sleep lasted six hours, eliminated the tiredness caused by working, and refreshed the sleeper. He recommended sleeping neither too much nor too little, but rather following the course of the sun, rising with it and going to bed at sunset.

In the seventeenth and eighteenth centuries sleep was often explained by a rather odd combination of physiological concepts and metaphysics. The British physician and physiologist Alexander Stuart thought, for example, that sleep resulted from a deficit of the "animal spirits," which work and motion drained from the body and eventually exhausted.* Sleep occurs because the fluid, or "liquor," in the brain cannot move freely; as it is gradually used up, it can no longer fill the small vessels and nerves that run from the brain to the sensory organs and voluntary muscles. These ideas of Boerhaave's bear a certain resemblance to the theories of the Swiss physician and naturalist Albrecht von Haller (1708–1777), who thought that thickened blood in the head created pressure on the brain, thereby cutting off the flow of the "spirits" to the nerves. The recent discovery

*For the Dutch physician Herman Boerhaave the *spiritus nervosi* are separated out of the blood by the brain.

of oxygen played an important role in the thinking of the German physiologist Jacob Fidelis Ackermann (1765–1815). He held that the oxygen in the air we inhale gives off an "ether of life," which reaches the brain by way of the blood and is there extracted and stored. Impelled by the "forces of the brain" into nerves and muscles, it produces "animal motion." Tiredness leads to a deficiency in the life ether; however, during sleep its supply can be replenished.

The kind of natural philosophy that arose in the nineteenth century brought mystical notions into fashion for a time. The views of Philipp Franz von Walther, a professor of physiology and surgery, may serve as an example: "Sleep is a surrendering of the egotistical being to the common life of the natural spirit, a flowing together of the individual human soul with the universal soul of nature."[9]

The growth of the natural sciences in the course of the nineteenth century led to theories that attempted to provide explanations for sleep based solely on the principles of physiology and chemistry. Alexander von Humboldt, for instance, believed that sleep was caused by a lack of oxygen, while the physiologist Eduard Friedrich Wilhelm Pflüger of Bonn thought it arose from a reduction in the amount of oxygen absorbed by "living brain molecules." Others ascribed the main cause of sleep to a lack of blood in the cortex of the brain, a swelling of nerve cells, and shifts in electric charges in the ganglia. In the second half of the last century, the German physiologist Wilhelm Thierry Preyer advanced the theory that tiredness creates substances in the body that absorb oxygen from the blood, thereby depriving the brain of the oxygen it needs to function actively. Preyer believed that he had identified these substances as lactic acid and creatine.

Although all of these theories made use of new scientific concepts to explain sleep, none of them were based on solid evidence, and their proponents did not generally attempt to test them in experiments. This task remained for the scientists of our century. In the following chapters, particularly in chapters 8 and 9, we will return to these scientific developments.

Places and Times for Sleeping: The Sociology of Sleep

In our part of the world most dwellings contain bedrooms, that is, special rooms for sleeping in.[10] This is a relatively recent phenomenon, however. Even in the late Middle Ages in Europe many people often still slept in one large room that not only was a bedroom but also served other purposes. Servants often slept in the vicinity of their masters, in order to be available to perform tasks for them at all hours. Separate rooms especially for sleeping first appeared in Europe at the courts of royalty. One of the most famous of these bedrooms belonged to the Sun King of France, Louis XIV; not only was it situated in the middle of the palace itself, but it was also a kind of center of power from which the king reigned. The *lever du roi* each morning, the ceremony at which the king held audience while still lying in bed, constituted the most important social event of the court day. The custom of having a separate bedroom was then taken over by the aristocracy; it did not appear in middle-class homes until later.

Arrangements for sleeping occasionally presented problems even in the inns of earlier days. The German sociologist Peter Gleichmann, for instance, reports on German spas of the seventeenth century where "half of the inn guests slept only until midnight because of a lack of beds; then the other half, who had been entertaining themselves with various activities until then, appeared to sleep in their turn."[11] In rural areas old sleeping habits died hard. Gleichmann quotes from a report on Breton farmers in the nineteenth century; among other things it describes how all family members and servants usually slept in one large bed. Travelers passing through were offered hospitality in the form of a place in the same, shared bed.

The increasing social segregation of men and women in the nineteenth century can also be observed in sleeping customs. In wealthy families the master and mistress of the house often had separate dressing rooms, while the children had their own nursery. Sometimes a "sons' room" existed as well as one for the daughters. Bedrooms that had formerly been relatively public rooms and easy of access were now closed off, belonging more and more to the private sphere. Changing attitudes are also reflected in arrangements in inns and hospitals, where common sleeping quarters became more infrequent and single rooms were on the rise.

Not only was the place for sleeping less rigidly prescribed in former times than nowadays, but also the time. Gleichmann notes illustrations dating from the end of the Middle Ages—in paintings of the Flemish school, for instance—in which people are often depicted sleeping in the daytime, next to houses and roads, or in fields. Even today travelers to countries like India are often struck by the number of people who can be seen sleeping outdoors during the day. In Europe and the West, by contrast, the attitude rapidly gained ground that it was inappropriate to sleep at certain times of day or in certain places. For example, sleeping in the streets or other public places is regarded as a breach of order, and the sleeper must reckon with being wakened by the police and sent on his way. In large cities like Paris the vagrants' custom of sleeping under bridges or in subway stations is only just tolerated. On the other hand, it is considered perfectly permissible for people of higher social standing to doze off while using public transportation such as trains or airplanes.

Sleeping in the daytime, which for us has become a symbol of laziness and shiftlessness, was a subject of the famous nineteenth-century Russian novel *Oblomov,* by Ivan Goncharov, and has achieved the status of a classic of world literature at least:

Lying down was not a necessity for Oblomov, as it is for a man who is sick or sleepy; or a matter of chance, as it is for one who is tired; or even the pleasure it is for a sluggard: it was his normal state. When he was at home—and he was rarely not at home—he was always lying down, always in the same room in which we found him, a room that served as bedroom, study, and reception room.[12]

The hero of the novel spends his entire life in bed, while his friends try in vain to convince him of the advantages of working.

The points raised in this chapter are intended to suggest, at least in outline, that nonscientific aspects of the subject of sleep are both interesting and instructive, whether they relate to cultural history, linguistics, sociology, or other fields. The following chapters will be concerned with developments in modern sleep research, which occurs for the most part within the framework of the natural sciences.

2

Scientists Investigate Sleep: The Different Stages of Sleep

> During sleep trains of waves appear which cannot be cor-
> related with any detectable external stimulus, but which
> may be connected with internal disturbances of unknown
> origin.
>
> —A. L. Loomis, E. N. Harvey, G. Hobart
> *Science* 81 (1935)

The Beginnings of Sleep Research

It is not surprising that until recently very few scientists regarded sleep as a rewarding subject for research. In contrast to
the waking state, which is accessible to observation and measurement and about which the subject of the experiment can
himself provide information, sleep appears to be largely an
inaccessible phenomenon. It is, of course, possible to observe
changes in the position of a sleeping person's body or to record
his breathing rate, his pulse, and his body temperature during
sleep. Such observations and measurements refer only to physical phenomena accompanying sleep, however, and say nothing
about the basic process itself. On the other hand, if the goal of

an experiment is to learn about the depth of a subject's sleep, then waking him with specific stimuli, or at least disturbing him as he sleeps, becomes unavoidable. The phenomenon under investigation, sleep, is therefore influenced by the experiment itself. Nevertheless, studies of this sort provided the first indications that sleep proceeds in progressive stages. A German physiologist named Kohlschütter established in the nineteenth century that sleep is deepest in the first few hours and becomes more superficial as time goes on. The greatest breakthrough for the development of modern research on sleep, however, was the discovery that electrical waves arise in the brain and can be continuously recorded.

Today in thousands of laboratories and hospitals all over the world patterns of electrical brain waves known as electroencephalograms (EEGs) are routinely recorded; yet this technique, which we have come to take for granted, is only fifty years old.

The Discovery of the EEG

In the 1920s the first experiments to record brain waves from the scalp were undertaken by Hans Berger. Dr. Berger, who at that time was head of the Neurology Department at the County Hospital in Jena, Germany, had a reputation as a quiet and respectable physician. He pursued his more unconventional scientific interests in his free time, after a day spent treating patients at the hospital. He devised experiments to test whether brain waves could be recorded from the scalp using equipment that by present-day standards was extremely primitive: an Edelmann galvanometer and later a Siemens coil galvanometer. Small silver plates that he attached to his subjects' heads served as electrodes. The electric currents that he was able to register with this procedure were scarcely larger than the fluctuations caused by his own inadequate equipment. Nevertheless he succeeded in recording, with relaxed but alert subjects, regular

waves of approximately ten cycles per second; these are generally known today as alpha rhythm.

At first Berger's work was either simply ignored by the medical profession or else treated with great suspicion. It was not
until his experiments were confirmed by the respected physiologists Adrian and Matthews in 1934 that his discoveries received the recognition they deserved.

Now let us take a look at how today, fifty years later, EEG
recordings are used in sleep research.

A Night in the Sleep Laboratory

Rebecca is a student who has often served as a subject for sleep
experiments and who is interested in this field of research herself. When she is awake, her alpha rhythm is quite distinct, and
the changes that occur when she falls asleep are clearly visible.
This facilitates an evaluation of the readings and makes her an
excellent subject. Rebecca has come today to get accustomed to
the laboratory during the first night, which will then be followed by several other nights in the course of the experiment.
She puts on her pajamas and takes a seat in a comfortable chair
so that the EEG electrodes can be affixed. Small plate-shaped
silver discs, each connected to a thin flexible cable, are filled
with a paste that will conduct electricity and are pressed on to
certain parts of her scalp. These electrodes register the EEG.
Two more are attached to the skin underneath her chin, where
they will pick up the electrical activity of the chin muscles.
(This record is called an electromyogram, or EMG.) The EMG
provides information about muscle tension or relaxation. Finally, electrodes are affixed near the outer corners of her eyes,
in order to record the electrical signals that occur when the eyes
move. This is the so-called electrooculogram, or EOG. As we
shall see, the EOG is especially important in recognizing a particular phase of sleep. After three-quarters of an hour all the

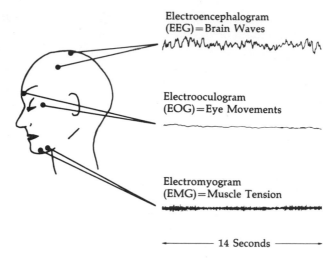

Electroencephalogram
(EEG)=Brain Waves

Electrooculogram
(EOG)=Eye Movements

Electromyogram
(EMG)=Muscle Tension

————— 14 Seconds —————

FIGURE 2.1
EEG, EOG, and EMG

Electrical waves provide information about sleep. The electroencephalogram is the record of electrical brain waves; the electrooculogram records
electric currents arising from movement of the eyes; the electromyogram
records currents that indicate the level of muscle tension.

electrodes have been put in place and the electrical contact with
the surface of the head has been tested. Now Rebecca enters the
comfortably furnished and soundproofed room in the laboratory where she will spend the night. After she has gotten into
bed, each cable running from an electrode is plugged into the
appropriate socket in a panel above the bed, so that she is
hooked up to the recording equipment. In this way signals can
be registered during the night from the next room. In spite of
the many cables attached to her head, Rebecca has enough
freedom of movement to be able to assume her normal sleeping
position and to be comfortable in bed. The experimenter wishes
her a good night's sleep and turns off the light. After a last check
of the settings on the equipment, he sets the paper drive going.
The paper begins to advance with a precisely determined speed
of ten millimeters per second. The pens of the polygraph start

to move, recording the EEG, EMG, and EOG as curves on the paper. The recording of Rebecca's sleep has begun.

The EEG During Wakefulness and Sleep

Even for a trained sleep researcher it is always fascinating to observe the ongoing recording of sleep. Looking at the continuously changing pattern of waves, the experimenter feels in direct contact with the progress of the subject's sleep. As he or she falls asleep, the regular alpha rhythm of the waking state changes to small and rapid oscillations. Then, as sleep continues, the EEG shifts gradually to larger and slower waves, which finally become the dominant pattern. As long ago as the 1930s the American physiologists Loomis and Davis and their colleagues observed these typical changes in the EEG during sleep and established that as the waves increased in size and slowed down, the subject's sleep became deeper. On the basis of these results they attempted to classify sleep into various stages. Their knowledge of the EEG changes occurring during sleep was incomplete, however, since one of the most important stages of sleep had not yet been discovered.

The Discovery of REM Sleep

The man who is rightly seen as the grandfather of modern sleep research is Nathaniel Kleitman. Now over ninety years old, he emigrated from his native Russia during World War I and settled in Chicago, where he devoted himself to experimental and theoretical sleep research. His book *Sleep and Wakefulness,* first published in 1939 and revised in 1963, contains more than four thousand references to the literature and is still a classic of sleep research. In 1952 Kleitman became interested in the slow, roll-

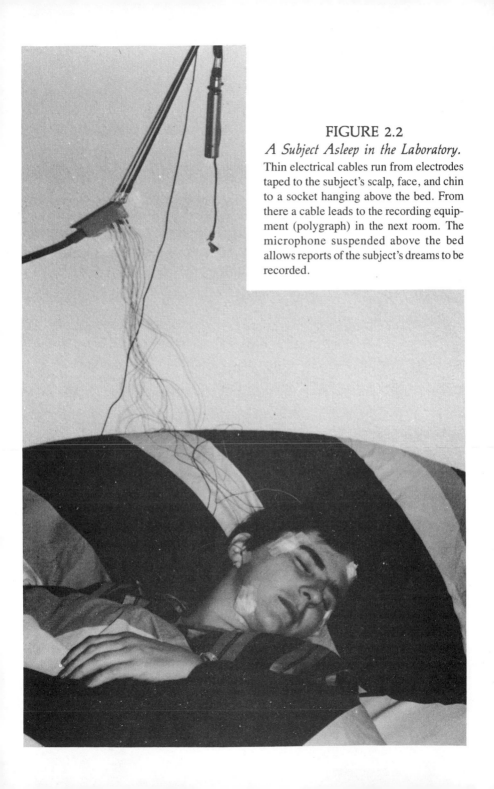

FIGURE 2.2
A Subject Asleep in the Laboratory.
Thin electrical cables run from electrodes taped to the subject's scalp, face, and chin to a socket hanging above the bed. From there a cable leads to the recording equipment (polygraph) in the next room. The microphone suspended above the bed allows reports of the subject's dreams to be recorded.

ing-eye movements that typically accompany the onset of sleep, and assigned one of his graduate students, Eugene Aserinsky, the task of making a closer study of this phenomenon. The eye movements were recorded, as has already been mentioned, by placing electrodes on the skin of the face directly next to the eyes and recording the electrooculogram (EOG). To his great surprise Aserinsky observed changes in the EOG long after subjects had fallen asleep; they looked like sudden occurrences of very rapid eye movements. These unexpected results were received with understandable skepticism by Professor Kleitman, since up to that time rapid eye movements had been known to occur only when people were awake and changed the direction in which they were looking. Nevertheless, direct observation of sleeping subjects confirmed that their eyes really were moving beneath closed lids. William Dement, who was then one of Kleitman's students and later went on to become a pioneer of modern research in the field, began a systematic investigation of this phenomenon. In the following years, Dement found that if subjects were awakened during a phase of sleep in which rapid eye movements occurred, they often reported that they had been dreaming. Several more years had to pass before it was realized that rapid eye movements during sleep were more than a marginal curiosity. In fact, a fundamental new stage of sleep had been discovered. The occurrence of eye movements in this stage led to the term *REM* (Rapid Eye Movement) *sleep,* which is in standard use today.

The Different Stages of Sleep—The Sleep Profile

We left Rebecca, the subject of our experiment, as the recording of her sleep was beginning. Let us now take a look over the experimenter's shoulder, at the wave patterns being recorded on paper. She has obviously not fallen asleep yet, since the EEG shows the typical alpha rhythm of the relaxed waking state.

The EOG is irregular, because her eyes are moving, and the rapid waves of the EMG indicate a high level of muscle tension. The picture changes after only a few minutes, as the alpha rhythm of the EEG gives way to small, rapid, and irregular waves, while the EOG shows slow oscillations corresponding to rolling movements of her eyes: Rebecca is falling asleep. She is in stage 1, a transitional phase between waking and sleeping. Shortly thereafter slightly larger waves appear, overlapping with bursts of rapid waves called sleep spindles. The pattern also shows the occasional appearance of large, slow waves: the so-called K-complexes. Muscle tension is significantly lower now than in the waking state, and the eyes are quiet. These are characteristic signs of stage 2, the first appearance of which is considered by many scientists to mark the actual onset of sleep. Stage 2 is an extremely important kind of sleep, since it takes up more than half of the total time spent sleeping.

After a further few minutes the EEG waves become still larger (of higher amplitude) and slower. These slow oscillations, which have a frequency of one to four cycles per second, are called delta waves. If they occupy between 20 and 50 percent of the recording time, then the sleeper is in stage 3. If they represent more than 50 percent, then sleep has reached stage 4. Stages 3 and 4 taken together are often considered to constitute "delta sleep," or deep sleep (see figure 2.3). Rebecca has now spent twenty minutes in stage 4. The EMG continues to register low muscle tension, and her eyes are still. But then the picture suddenly changes. The EMG rises, with the polygraph pen vibrating so rapidly that it splatters ink on the paper. The pen of the EEG channel swings across to its farthest possible extension, and for a few seconds no recognizable pattern exists at all. What has happened? The subject has shifted position in her sleep, causing electrical disturbances in the registration. Although such body movements are infrequent as sleep becomes progressively deeper (in the transition from stage 2 to stages 3 and 4), they occur quite often at the end of a period of deep sleep. Stage 2 sleep follows for several minutes after this brief

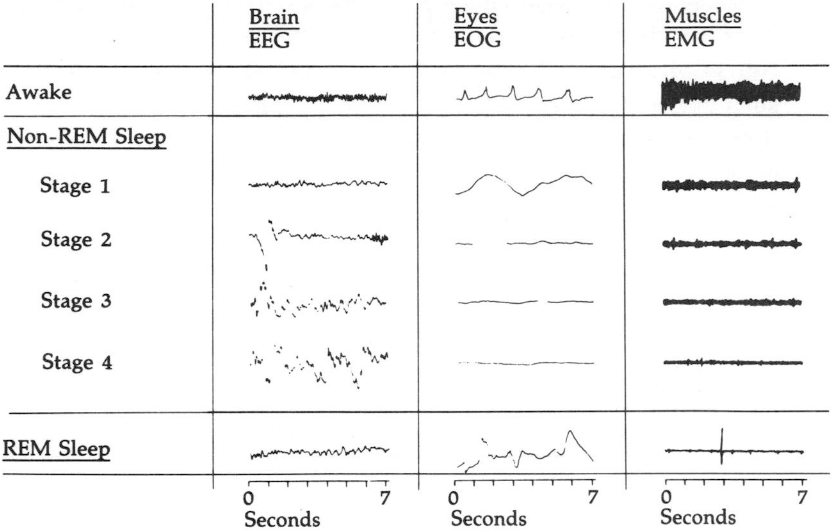

	Brain EEG	Eyes EOG	Muscles EMG
Awake			
Non-REM Sleep			
Stage 1			
Stage 2			
Stage 3			
Stage 4			
REM Sleep			
	0 7 Seconds	0 7 Seconds	0 7 Seconds

FIGURE 2.3
The Stages of Sleep.

The stages of sleep are determined from patterns of electrical waves recorded from the brain, eyes, and muscles. As non-REM sleep increases in depth (from stage 1 to stage 4), the brain waves (EEG) become larger and slower; at the same time muscle tension drops. As sleep begins (stage 1), slow rolling-eye movements occur. During REM sleep the EEG resembles that of stage 1, but the EOG registers the typical rapid eye movements. The EMG registers an occasional muscle twitch, but otherwise the muscles are completely relaxed.

episode of body movement. Then, however, the EMG line flattens out in a matter of seconds, indicating an almost complete disappearance of muscle tension. The EEG pattern now resembles that of the first, transitional stage 1 and shows small, rapid oscillations. The EOG channel registers the distinct waves that correspond to rapid eye movements. Rebecca has reached the first period of REM sleep, which lasts for only a few minutes, however, to be followed by more stage 2 sleep. A new cycle has thus begun. Once again her sleep proceeds through stages 3 and 4, after which a second period of REM sleep occurs. In the course of a full night's sleep, we can distinguish four to five such cycles. Deep sleep (stages 3 and 4) appears clearly in the first two of these cycles; thereafter it occurs only very briefly or is no longer present at all. The reverse is true for the REM sleep periods, which increase in length from cycle to cycle. The two states, deep sleep and REM sleep, thus show opposite tendencies in the course of a night.

The discovery of REM sleep so fascinated scientists that this stage became the focus of most sleep experiments. The other sleep state (stages 1 to 4), which had been known for a much longer time, received the rather uninspired name of non-REM sleep. A full sleep cycle therefore consists of a sequence of a non-REM and a REM sleep period. A typical non-REM/REM

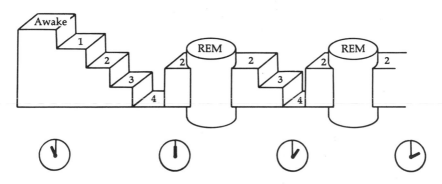

FIGURE 2.4

The "Sleep Staircase" During the First Three Hours of the Night.
Each stair corresponds to a level of sleep. After falling asleep, one "descends" through stage 2 into deep sleep (stages 3 and 4). The first REM sleep episode occurs just over an hour later. Since REM sleep is fundamentally different from non-REM sleep, it is shown as a column. Although the EEG during REM sleep resembles that of the early transitional stage 1, REM sleep is nonetheless deep. For this reason REM sleep is often called paradoxical sleep. Non-REM and REM sleep follow one another in a cyclical pattern. In this diagram only two complete cycles are shown.

cycle lasts about ninety minutes. As we shall see, this cyclical sequence of stages is a highly characteristic feature of sleep which is not restricted to the sleep of human beings.

The EEG varies from subject to subject. Some people show a pattern of large (high-amplitude) waves during deep sleep, while the pattern in others is flatter. The alpha rhythm may be quite distinct or barely discernible. In order to be able to compare different experiments in spite of such individual variations, a group of American scientists devised a set of criteria that have since been generally applied to define the sleep stages. The definitions of non-REM stages 1 to 4 and REM sleep are now scored according to the criteria established by Rechtschaffen and Kales. An experienced experimenter needs about an hour to determine the sleep stage for consecutive thirty-second intervals during a night-long sleep experiment. When he is finished, he has reviewed quite a considerable amount of paper, for the EEG record of a whole night is approximately three hundred yards long.

Spectral Analysis of a Sleep EEG

We divide sleep into five stages according to the above-mentioned definitions. Stages 1 to 4 of non-REM sleep succeed one another without distinct demarcations, however, so that the stage divisions represent fairly arbitrary categories. We can demonstrate this most clearly by performing a spectral analysis of an entire night's EEG, a procedure that also shows that changes may occur within an individual sleep stage.

The EEG consists of an irregular pattern of both slow and rapid waves. Biologists have begun to use a technique called spectral analysis, which permits the dissection of a signal such as an EEG into its frequency components. The spectrum indicates what percentage of the whole signal consists of rapid or slow oscillations. Thus spectral analysis of an EEG provides

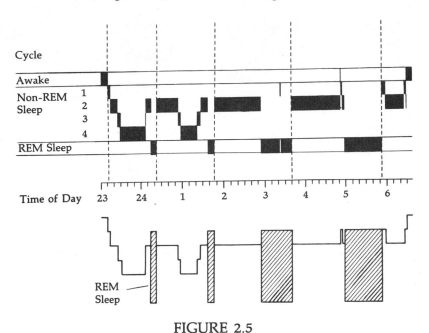

FIGURE 2.5

The Sleep Profile of a Whole Night.

Onset of sleep: 11:10 P.M.; awakening: 6:30 A.M. At the bottom is a "sleep staircase" similar to the one in figure 2.4. Above is a sleep profile as it is usually depicted. Four complete non-REM/REM sleep cycles are demarcated by vertical dotted lines. Deep sleep (stages 3 and 4) occurs only in the first two cycles. The increased length of REM sleep episodes in the second half of the night is typical.

information about whether slow waves (of low frequency) or rapid waves (of high frequency) predominate at any given moment. A new method developed at the Laboratory for Experimental and Clinical Sleep Research at the University of Zurich allows us to compute EEG spectra for consecutive periods of one minute. When such measurements are taken during an entire night, the changes in the EEG can be graphically displayed and related to the stages of sleep. We use a computer installed in the laboratory that can compute spectra from approximately 500,000 data points sampled from the EEG.

As figure 2.6 shows, the onset of sleep is followed by a slow

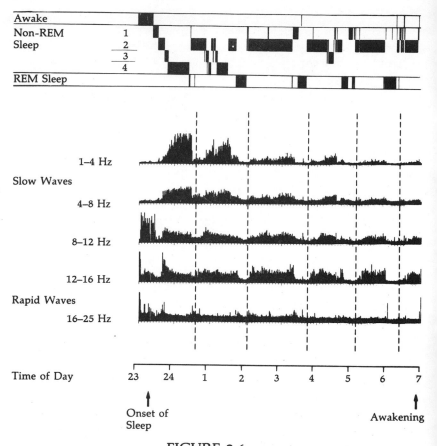

FIGURE 2.6

Stages of Sleep and EEG Spectra of a Whole Night.

EEG spectra permit exact measurement of the changes during sleep. The top part of the diagram shows a sleep profile similar to the one in figure 2.5. The lower part contains spectral patterns for slow (1–8 Hz), medium (8–12 Hz), and rapid EEG waves (12–25 Hz). High values indicate that the percentage of waves in a particular frequency range is high. For example, the percentage of very slow waves rises as deep non-REM sleep increases, reaching a peak in stage 4. Spectral analysis reveals that changes in sleep do not actually occur with abrupt shifts in level as in a staircase but are gradual and continuous instead. The division of sleep into stages is thus only a rough approximation of real changes. (Hz is the abbreviation for Hertz — number of oscillations per second.)

increase of EEG activity in the low-frequency bands (slow waves); the phases in which these waves reach their peak correspond to periods of deep sleep (stages 3 and 4). One can clearly observe that the height of the peaks decreases during the course of the night. In this figure the "valleys" correspond to REM sleep. In the frequency band 8–12 Hz, which represents the alpha rhythm of relaxed wakefulness, the highest levels occur before the onset of sleep. (Hertz, abbreviated Hz, is a measure for the number of oscillations per second of a signal.) Activity in the region of 12–16 Hz corresponds in part to the sleep spindles (sporadic rapid waves) characteristic of stage 2. This band shows high levels during non-REM sleep and low levels during REM sleep. In the highest frequency band, from 16 to 25 Hz, almost no stage-related changes are visible.

In summary we can conclude that changes in the spectrum correspond in large measure to the sleep profile based on Rechtschaffen and Kales's definitions of sleep stages, even though spectral analysis does not include EOG and EMG measurements. It follows that the EEG is an excellent indicator of changes occurring in the brain during sleep. The processes that generate EEG patterns are not yet fully understood, however. It is currently assumed that the EEG is caused primarily by currents in the cortex of the brain that arise at the junctions of nerve cells (synapses). Since many nerve cells and nerve fibers (axons) run in a parallel direction, thousands of individual electric potentials summate and can be recorded from the scalp as brain waves.

Body Functions During Sleep

We have concentrated until now on the EEG, because this signal most clearly reflects the changes in our sleeping state. Alterations in muscle tension and eye movements have also been mentioned. But what about other body functions?

As we fall asleep, many processes in our body are "put on the back burner," as it were. Our body temperature sinks a few tenths of a degree, our breathing and pulse rates decrease, and our blood pressure drops. Measurements of the "stress hormone" cortisol, which is produced in the cortex of the adrenal glands, reveal lower levels during sleep than in a preceding waking state. The situation is just the reverse for the growth hormone, which reaches extremely high levels during the first stage of deep sleep. It is possible that these hormonal changes that follow upon the onset of sleep cause an activation of anabolic processes in the metabolism.

In contrast to non-REM sleep, REM sleep is accompanied by increased activity in body functions. As a period of REM sleep begins, breathing becomes irregular, and the pulse and blood pressure exhibit brief episodes of fluctuations as well. A further typical phenomenon in this stage of sleep among males is the erection of the penis. This was described in the 1940s but not systematically studied until after the discovery of REM sleep. An apparatus that can measure changes in the volume of the penis (phallus) makes it possible to record a "phallogram" simultaneously with the EEG. Erections in sleep occur not only in adults but also in children and even infants. Phallograms are used today in clinical medicine for diagnostic purposes: they can help determine whether impotence has an organic cause (for example, an impairment of the nerves) or is of psychological origin. The latter type of impotence does not prevent the occurrence of erections during sleep. Quite awhile before we wake up, certain signs herald the end of sleep: both body temperature and the level of cortisol begin to rise, and the sleeper changes position more often. It looks as if during the last part of sleep the organism is slowly getting ready to spend some time awake again.

3

Sleep: A Theme with Variations

Lausius—an ancient poet—decrees five hours' sleep for the young man and the graybeard, six for the merchant, seven for aristocrats, and for the lazy and wholly idle man eight hours.

—Heinrich Nudow
Versuch einer Theorie des Schlafs (1791)

Sleep at Different Stages of Life

A baby spends two-thirds of its time asleep in the first few days after birth. It wakes up at intervals of two to six hours, drinks its milk, and goes back to sleep. Its sleep is distributed almost evenly over a twenty-four-hour period. Luckily this state of affairs, which often robs worn-out parents of their much-needed rest, tends not to last long. A three-month-old infant seldom wakes up during the night; at the age of six months it is still sleeping about twelve hours a day but is also awake for long periods at a stretch.

The amount of time spent sleeping during the day decreases in the early years of a child's life. Although most preschool children still take an afternoon nap, when they reach school age they stay awake for the whole day. The so-called polyphasic (multiphase) sleep pattern of the newborn infant has changed into the monophasic (single-phase) pattern of the adult.

Sleep at Different Stages in Life

What do the different stages of sleep look like in an infant? In the early months of life an infant's sleep is equally divided between REM and non-REM sleep. The REM sleep of a baby resembles that of an adult in many respects. Rapid eye move-

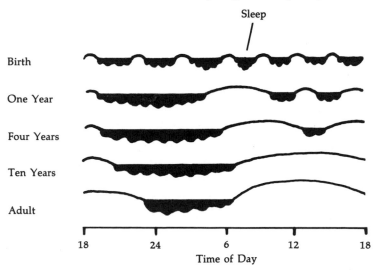

FIGURE 3.1
As a Child Develops, Its Sleep Gradually Becomes Restricted to the Night.

Polyphasic (multiphase) sleep following birth changes first to biphasic (two-phase) sleep among preschool children and later to monophasic (single-phase) sleep. Among the elderly, periods of sleep during the day become more frequent again.

SOURCE: Adapted from N. Kleitman, *Sleep and Wakefulness,* 2nd Edition (Chicago: University of Chicago Press, 1963).

ments occur sporadically; tension of the voluntary muscles is greatly reduced; respiration rate and pulse are irregular. In contrast to adult patterns, however, the EEG of an infant during REM sleep hardly differs from its waking EEG. An infant in a REM sleep period is also much more restless than an adult. Its arms and legs move constantly, as do the muscles of its face. Premature babies, in particular, are so active that it is difficult to tell whether they are in a REM sleep period or awake. During this early stage of development scientists speak of "active sleep," in contrast to the "quiet sleep" without eye and body movements that corresponds to non-REM sleep. The sequence of sleep stages differs as well: newborn babies often enter REM sleep immediately following wakefulness, a phenomenon that is rare in adults. Babies are usually two to three months old before they develop the sequence wakefulness/non-REM sleep/REM sleep, which they will retain for the rest of their lives.

As figure 3.2 shows, the percentage of REM sleep decreases rapidly in the first few months of an infant's life. The REM sleep of a two- to three-year-old toddler has already been reduced to 25 percent of the total recording time, that is, to a level not significantly different from that of an adult.

But what about deep sleep? A newborn baby produces an EEG pattern of mixed slow and rapid waves during non-REM sleep to begin with; but after a few months it is replaced by continuous slow waves. By the age of three months an infant spends the first few hours of the night in deep sleep, so that its sequence of sleep stages corresponds more closely to those of adult sleep.

A final point remains to be mentioned concerning the cycle of non-REM/REM sleep. While the whole cycle can be observed in small children, it is of shorter duration: forty-five to fifty minutes for a one-year-old, increasing to sixty to seventy minutes in children between the ages of five and ten. Older children then gradually develop the ninety-minute cycle typical

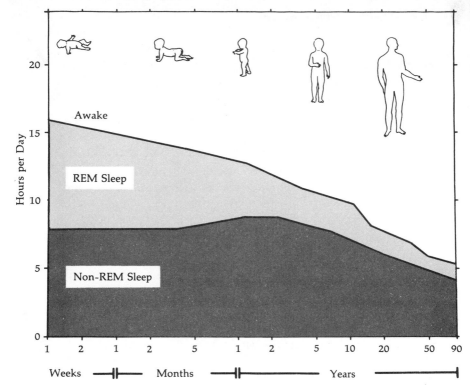

FIGURE 3.2

The Distribution of Sleep Stages Is Dependent upon Age.

Half of a newborn infant's sleep consists of REM sleep. During the first
year of life the length of REM sleep is drastically reduced, whereas the
length of non-REM sleep remains almost constant. Among adults the
percentage of REM sleep in the total sleep period is only 20–25 percent.
Since this diagram is based on findings made in a sleep laboratory, the total
length of sleep observed for adult age groups is too short in comparison
with results obtained from surveys. It has also not been definitely shown
that the total length of sleep is shorter for those in the highest age group
than for young adults. It should be noted that the table depicts age loga-
rithmically, i.e., time in years is shown in an increasingly compressed
manner.

SOURCE: Adapted from H. P. Roffwarg; J. N. Muzio; and C. W. Dement,
"Ontogenetic Development of the Human Sleep-Dream Cycle," *Science*
152 (29 September 1966: 604–19). Copyright 1966 by the American
Association for the Advancement of Science.

of adults. In summary we can say that some essential features of adult sleep patterns are already present in early childhood. As children grow, they tend to sleep less during the day, and the total amount of time they spend asleep decreases. The percentage of REM sleep drops from 50 percent to less than 25 percent.

The sleep of young and middle-aged adults will occupy us in later chapters; for the moment it should be pointed out that the monophasic pattern of sleep described above is not always the rule and is often the result of cultural traditions. In northern and central Europe and in North America, for instance, working adults rarely take afternoon naps, although this is common in Mediterranean countries and many parts of Central and South America. The custom of the "siesta" permits people in southern countries to avoid the greatest heat of the day and spend this time sleeping. They can return refreshed to work and pleasure in the cooler hours of the evening and night. In a recent study by the Greek sleep researcher Constantin Soldatos in Athens, 42 percent of the people polled said that they took a siesta at least three times a week, lasting on the average just over an hour. Soldatos comes to the conclusion that this formerly widespread custom is on the decline in Greece—that more and more people are doing without this rest time, either voluntarily or involuntarily.

Climatic conditions can therefore cause adults to maintain the biphasic (two-phase) sleep characteristic of preschool children. It is interesting to note that in present-day China the custom of the siesta (called *xiu-xi*) is widely observed. Employees in factories and offices regularly lie down for naps after the lunch break. Article 49 of the Chinese constitution establishes that "the working population has a right to rest." Shiyi Liu, a Chinese specialist on sleep research from the Academy of Sciences in Shanghai, was concerned about what he observed during a stay in Europe. He remarked to me, "People in the West get too little sleep. In Germany students go to discos several times a week and stay up until the small hours. Where is this going to lead?"

Elderly people tend to sleep during the day even in our part of the world. Inge Strauch, a professor of clinical psychology at the University of Zurich who is engaged in sleep research, conducted a poll of people between the ages of sixty-five and eighty-three and found that 60 percent of them took frequent or daily naps. Increased sleep in the daytime leads to a reduction of sleep at night. Whether total sleeping time decreases in old age is not yet clear. Elderly people tend to nod off frequently during the day and wake up repeatedly in the night; this multiphasic sleep bears a certain resemblance to the sleep patterns of small children.

Changes in the sleep/wake cycle are also accompanied by changes in the stages of sleep and in the EEG patterns. Older people spend less time in deep sleep, and the slow waves characteristic of this stage (delta waves) are less pronounced. On the other hand the percentage of REM sleep remains relatively constant even in the higher age group (see figure 3.2).

As people grow old, they have increased difficulty sleeping: elderly people often spend a long time in bed unable to fall asleep; they have to get up to go to the toilet frequently and tend to wake up very early in the morning, a phenomenon that is sometimes jokingly referred to as "senile bed evasion." Nonetheless, they generally feel rested and, in contrast to many younger people, do not mind getting up early. However, the fact that many old people get up early without difficulty does not necessarily imply that they are all satisfied with their sleep. On the contrary, complaints about poor sleep increase drastically in old age, as has already been mentioned, and are reflected in the high consumption of sleeping pills among persons in this age group. But whether frequently interrupted sleep, which is often experienced as unsatisfactory, should be considered as a normal part of the aging process or rather as the result of disease and pathological changes in the organism is a difficult question to answer.

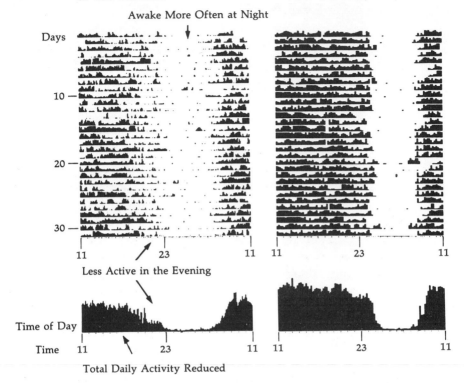

FIGURE 3.3

Elderly People Wake Up More Frequently at Night.

The rest-activity cycles of a sixty-six-year-old man (retired) and a forty-four-year-old man (with full-time employment) were recorded continuously for one month. Every horizontal line represents one twenty-four-hour day. Peaks during the day correspond to high physical activity; empty spaces in between correspond to rest periods. The chart of the younger man (on the right) shows a high amount of daytime activity and pronounced periods of rest at night. The chart of the older man (on the left) reflects fewer long periods of daytime activity, and the total activity is clearly reduced in the evening hours. By contrast, his nighttime rest is more frequently interrupted by movements arising in part from waking and getting up during the night. Activity averaged over the course of the entire month is illustrated at the bottom. (From a study by M. Loepfe.)

Early Birds and Night Owls

"The early bird catches the worm," says the proverb. Going to bed early and starting the day's work early in the morning has long been considered a praiseworthy and virtuous way of life. "Early to bed and early to rise makes a man healthy, wealthy, and wise," runs another saying. Shakespeare has Juliet's nurse scold her, "Fie! you slug-abed!" when she finds her mistress still asleep (*Romeo and Juliet,* 4.5.2). Going to bed at an early hour has been held up to young people not only as morally superior but also as especially healthy. Prof. Theodor Stöckmann, a German school principal at the beginning of the century, instructed his charges in the theory of so-called natural sleep. He believed that sleep before midnight had twice the restorative power of sleep occurring after the witching hour. He also claimed that a person could easily get along on only four to five hours sleep a night if he went to bed at 7 P.M. Stöckmann and his followers cited many individual instances to prove their case for natural sleep, but serious scientific studies to back it up are still lacking. The opinion—which can still often be met with—that sleep in the hours before midnight is particularly healthy has not been definitely confirmed in experiments. Nevertheless, the time of day or night that one goes to bed is not unimportant. We shall return to this topic in connection with the discussion of biological rhythms.

Stöckmann's follower Georg Alfred Tienes writes, "Morning is the best and most suitable time for work, because we are then rejuvenated, more flexible and energetic, and more susceptible to stimulation; in short, we show more characteristics of youth."[1] But perhaps the reader belongs to just that category of people who have trouble joining in this paean to the early morning hours. People who have difficulty getting up and becoming cheerfully alert in the morning are often accused of having "got out on the wrong side of the bed." They continue to feel half-asleep after getting up; they drag and droop, do not have much appetite at the start of the day, and often eat very little breakfast or none at all. As the morning wears on, they still do not feel at their best, reacting to those around them in monosyllables and in a grumpy tone. By afternoon their physical state and mood start to improve, so that they gradually feel more dynamic and capable of sustained effort. People of this type do their best work in the evening and often have no trouble staying awake and active into the small hours of the morning.

Sleep specialists refer to these kind of people as "evening types." They stand in direct contrast to pronounced "morning types," who correspond most closely to the doctrines of Stöckmann and Tienes. Morning types wake up by themselves and get up without difficulty, feeling rested and fresh, and are able to work most efficiently in the hours before noon. Their energy declines by late afternoon, their tiredness increases, and, if circumstances permit it, they go to bed early.

The English sleep specialist Jim Horne and his Swedish colleague Olov Oestberg worked out a questionnaire to distinguish morning from evening types. They divided people into five categories: "definitely" morning or evening types, "moderately" morning or evening types, and "neither" types. In the sample that they studied, the pronounced morning types went to bed about an hour and a half earlier than the pronounced evening types and got up about two hours earlier.

Differences also occurred in their body temperature curves over the course of the day: morning types reached their temperature peak in the evening more than an hour before the evening types. The American sleep researchers Wilse Webb and Michael Bonnet came up with similar findings; they concluded, in addition, that morning types tend to sleep the same number of hours each night and that they enjoy a less problematic, more satisfying sleep than do evening types.

Scientific research on sleep did not deal with this set of questions until quite recently, and the results achieved up to now do not present a clear picture. But the characteristics of morning and evening types, and their distribution in the population, are an important topic for scientific investigation. This may be of great comfort to extreme evening types, who often encounter severe criticism and little sympathy in our society. The hours they keep are not a sign of "depravity," however, but merely represent one end of the scale in the statistical distribution of sleeping habits.

The question of why such different morning and evening types exist at all has not yet been answered. We still do not know how large a role inherited constitutional predispositions may play, or whether habits acquired in the course of a lifetime are the major factor. Certain indications suggest, however, that inherited tendencies may weigh more heavily.

Short and Long Sleepers

Napoleon needed extremely little sleep. He went to bed between 10 A.M. and midnight and slept until 2 A.M. Then he got up, worked in his study until about 5 A.M., and went back to bed again until 7 A.M. His opinion that only fools and invalids need more sleep is well known. Other famous short sleepers, who did not need more than four to six hours of sleep a night, are Edison and Churchill. The British statesman used to work until three or four in the morning and was up again by eight, but he did take a two-hour siesta in the afternoon. On the other hand, examples also exist of geniuses who were long sleepers: one of the most famous is Albert Einstein. He enjoyed spending ten hours a night in bed, where he is said to have discovered some crucial parts of his theory of relativity.

Short sleepers are particularly interesting subjects for research, since in their case the recuperative and restorative powers that sleep is supposed to possess—but which have not yet been sufficiently explained—are restricted to a relatively short time period. A story is told about the siestas of the Spanish painter Salvador Dali. He would sit in an armchair with a pewter plate on the floor next to him, holding a spoon between his thumb and index finger. He would lean back and relax, but as soon as he nodded off, the spoon would fall on the plate and wake him up. The sleep he enjoyed in this instant between falling asleep and awakening was said to have been so refreshing that Dali could go back to work feeling rested and energetic: a truly surrealistic afternoon nap!

Claims about extremely short sleep or the complete lack of sleep require careful checking. The Scottish sleep specialist and psychiatrist Ian Oswald recently reported the case of a man who claimed not to have slept at all for the preceding ten years. The man traced his sleeplessness back to an automobile accident, and he had received large payments in compensation for this "impairment of his health." During an investigation of his condition in a sleep laboratory, where he spent several days accompanied by his wife, he did in fact sleep for a total of only twenty minutes. But by the fourth day he was obviously so sleepy that he could hardly keep his eyes open. After managing to keep himself awake the following night until 6 A.M., he finally fell asleep and snored loudly until his wife woke him two and a half hours later. Even then he insisted on going back to sleep. This was a clear case of a short sleeper who, wanting to make some profit out of his disability at the insurance company's expense, had successfully feigned total sleeplessness over a period of years.

Apart from such false claims, however, verified instances of extremely short sleep can be found. Henry Jones and Ian Oswald examined two healthy Australian men, thirty and fifty-four years old, who claimed to need only three hours of sleep a night. Both held full-time jobs and appeared to lead active lives. The six to seven nights they spent in the sleep laboratory under observation confirmed that both slept an average of less than three hours per night. More than 50 percent of this time consisted of deep sleep (stages 3 and 4); REM sleep, which occurred soon after the onset of sleep, made up about 25 percent.

An even more extreme case of short sleep was reported by the English sleep researcher Ray Meddis and his colleagues. A seventy-year-old retired nurse stated that she could get along on only one hour's sleep a night. She simply did not feel tired and spent the night writing and painting. They conducted two series of laboratory tests of three and five nights to observe her; observation continued during the day to make sure that she did not go to bed then. The laboratory recordings once again confirmed the extremely brief sleep periods, and again deep sleep made up almost half the sleep time, a highly unusual phenomenon, given the advanced age of the subject. By contrast, the percentage of REM sleep was below the usual level of her age group. The report emphasizes that the subject remained in the best of moods during both series of experiments and that no signs of sleep deprivation could be observed.

Up to now we have been concerned with extreme cases of short sleep. How widespread is short sleep in the population at large? Figure 3.4 shows the statistical distribution of hours spent asleep. The graph is based on a poll of more than 800,000 Americans over the age of thirty. It is important to keep in mind that the material consisted solely of subjective answers that could not be verified by objective tests. Only one person in a thousand of those questioned claimed to sleep less than four hours, while four in a thousand said that they slept between four and five hours. At the other end of the scale, sixteen people per thousand slept more than ten hours. The peak of the distribution curve lay between eight and nine hours, a response given by 42 percent of the people polled. Approximately one-third of the sample gave the answer seven to eight hours. A more recent French survey (of 800 people) also found the most frequent response to be eight to eight and a half hours. Differences in the length of sleep occur not only in adults. The Children's Hospital

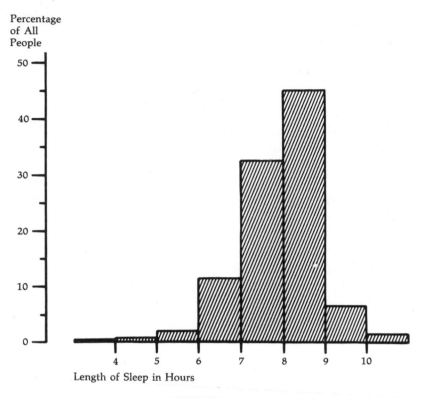

Percentage
of All
People

FIGURE 3.4
How Long Do People Sleep?

Most people sleep from seven to nine hours a night. The illustration rests on a survey of almost one million adults. A sleep duration of eight to nine hours was reported most often, followed by seven to eight hours. Only a tiny percentage reported that they slept less than four hours or more than ten.

Source: Based on data from D. F. Kripke et al., "Short and Long Sleep and Sleeping Pills: Is Increased Mortality Associated?," *Archives of General Psychiatry* 36 (1979):103–16.

of the University of Zurich conducted an investigation into the sleep of five-year-old children, which was shown to vary from eight to fifteen hours. How do such considerable differences arise? A Finnish research team recently tested the theory that inherited factors could determine the amount of sleep needed. Their study covered more than 2,000 identical twins, with identical genetic material, as well as 4,000 nonidentical twins, whose genetic material differed. The results showed that inherited factors affected to a statistically significant extent the length of sleep and even the subjective judgment of the quality of sleep. Identical twins produced similar values even when they lived apart from one another.

What has been said here about the length of time spent asleep is based on average values. Variations occurring in one and the same individual were ignored. We know very well from our own experience that we do not always sleep the same number of hours each night. External circumstances can play a role, permitting us to get a large amount of sleep in certain situations (on weekends or vacations, for instance) and very little in others (as when studying for an exam or taking care of someone who is sick). But internal factors are important as well. Changes in mood can strongly influence sleep: one can often hear that when people feel good and are in a cheerful mood they need less sleep than at times when they are depressed or worried. In short, we could say that each one of us has the potential to be a short or long sleeper.

Let us turn now to the sleep profile of short and long sleepers. The French physiologist and sleep expert Odile Benoit has made a special study of this field. Her most striking finding is that although long sleepers spend more time asleep, they have less deep sleep (stages 3 and 4) than do short sleepers. On the other hand, it was precisely the long sleepers who reacted to a period of sleep deprivation by increasing the length of their deep sleep in the first sleep cycle. These observations can be explained when we consider that long sleepers can reach the important stage of deep sleep during the first hours of the night. As they go on sleeping, they get their rest in "diluted" form (as stage 2 sleep). Short sleepers, however, are able to spend a longer time in deep sleep, which allows them to "fill their quota" within a shorter time.

Health and Length of Sleep

To conclude the subject of short and long sleep, we now turn to a fascinating study on the relationship between sleep length and health whose results pose more questions than they answer. Although sleep has been credited with health-giving powers since ancient times, this assumption has hardly ever been scientifically tested. Not long ago the American psychiatrist Dan Kripke and his associates published some relevant findings in connection with this question. Their evidence is based on a survey of more than a million adults over thirty that was carried out in the years 1959–60 by the American Cancer Society. Although the investigation was not primarily concerned with sleep, it asked questions about the length of sleep, the use of sleeping pills, and possible sleep disturbances. Six years after this poll a second study determined how many people in the survey had died in the meantime and of what causes. A surprising connection was revealed between the length of sleep and the mortality rate (see figure 3.5). The mortality rate was lowest among people who slept between seven and eight hours a night; it rose significantly among those who slept both less and more. (The mortality rate is the ratio of the actual number of deaths occurring and the statistically expected number of deaths in the general population.) In the illustration the results are expressed relative to the category with the lowest mortality rate (people who slept between seven and eight hours). The mortality rate was one and a half to two times higher among the group of extremely long sleepers (more than ten hours); it was almost two and a half times higher for extremely short sleepers (less than four hours) than for people who slept seven to eight hours. The reader will now probably want to know what the causes of death were in the groups with higher rates. The surprising answer: almost all causes of death were more prevalent. Short and long sleepers alike died more often of heart disease, cancer, and suicide. It should also be

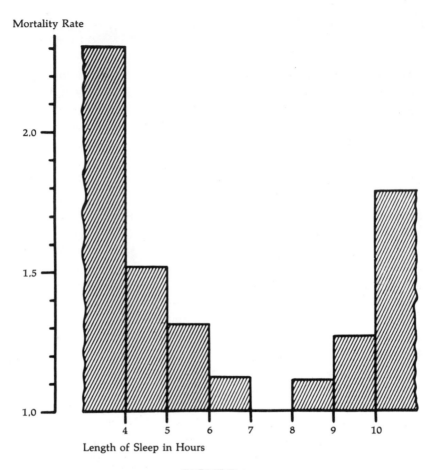

FIGURE 3.5
Mortality Rates.

The mortality rate is lowest among people who sleep between seven and eight hours per night. It increases progressively with shorter or longer sleep.

SOURCE: Based on data from D. F. Kripke et al., "Short and Long Sleep and Sleeping Pills: Is Increased Mortality Associated?," *Archives of General Psychiatry* 36 (1979):103–16.

mentioned incidentally that the mortality rate among frequent users of sleeping pills was double that of people who did not take medication in order to sleep.

How should these findings be interpreted? As a separate study showed, people who sleep less than seven or more than eight hours by no means lead a generally less healthy life (which is assessed by such items as smoking, alcohol consumption, excess weight, or insufficient exercise) than do their fellow citizens with seven to eight hours of rest a night. But the possibility cannot be excluded that external factors (such as stress or work on night shifts) or internal causes (the early stages of a disease) influence sleep, leading to an increase in the mortality rate. There need not therefore be a causal relationship between length of sleep and mortality rate. Nevertheless, it is not immediately clear why such external and internal causes should lead to opposite effects—namely, to both a shortening and a lengthening of sleep. The possibility remains that sleep exerts a beneficial influence on physical as well as mental health, the precise nature of which is still unknown; the results indicate that either too much or too little sleep is bad for you.

4

Dreams

If a man could pass thro' Paradise in a Dream, & have a flower presented to him as a pledge that his Soul had really been there, & found that flower in his hand when he awoke—Aye! and what then?

—Samuel Taylor Coleridge
The Notebooks, vol. 3

Dreams have fascinated and perturbed human beings since time began. When scientists discovered REM sleep and learned that dream experiences are connected with it, a new era in dream research opened up. But scientists often use strict, reductionist methods to interpret their findings, and where dreams are concerned this can lead to oversimplification, a danger that dream research has not always successfully avoided. In the following chapter we will start by describing some general characteristics of dreams and then go on to look at some questions concerning their origin and meaning. I have chosen not to limit the discussion to the results of experimental research but rather to approach the subject in a broader context.

"Ordinary" Dreams

When we speak of dreams, the first thing that tends to come to mind is the presence of unusual and fantastic events in them.

In our dreams we encounter people who have been dead for years. We suddenly find ourselves in far-off lands. Animals speak to us, and we ourselves possess powers that would strike us as completely impossible in waking life. If someone were to tell us that he had similar experiences when awake, we would doubt his sanity.

Let us begin by describing the most important characteristics of dreams more precisely. The dreamer finds himself in surroundings that often change abruptly, although sometimes a change of scene occurs more gradually. Scenes and people from our past appear. Obviously the laws of space and time are suspended in dreams. Another important trait of dreams is their riveting nature. Our attention is captured by certain events or objects, from which we cannot free it; we cannot choose to direct our thoughts to something else. The American sleep researcher Allan Rechtschaffen made the paradoxical but correct observation that dreams are lacking in imagination. When we dream, our mind does not wander, as it does when we are awake. The dream's images fill the dream entirely, and no room remains for other "reveries." This "single-mindedness" of dreams accounts for that peculiar feeling that dreams take place in a self-contained world of their own. Although other people appear in them, we feel fundamentally alone and cannot communicate our experiences to anyone else. We are entirely in the grip of the experience, unable to reflect on it or evaluate it. As a result we accept the most astonishing circumstances in dreams without surprise and never exclaim or protest, "But that's impossible!"

The following account of a dream, from an ancient Chinese text, illustrates strikingly the paradoxical closed world of dreams:

Once upon a time, I, Chuang Tzu, dreamt I was a butterfly, fluttering hither and thither, to all intents and purposes a butterfly. I was conscious only of following my fancies as a butterfly, and was unconscious of my individuality as a man.

Suddenly I awaked, and there I lay, myself again. Now I do not know whether I was a man dreaming I was a butterfly, or whether I am now a butterfly dreaming I am a man.[1]

Generally speaking, the world of dreams vanishes on awakening, leaving a vague memory at the very most. We are often aware in the morning of having had a dream, but cannot remember what it was about. If we recall that one to two hours of every night are spent in REM sleep, when dreams frequently occur, then the extent to which memory of the dream disappears seems quite remarkable. If we wake up just after dreaming about something and still have the images of this dream clearly in our minds, we find it difficult to describe those images, and our attempts to do so are seldom satisfactory. Even if we do succeed in giving an accurate account of what happened in our dream, it is still usually impossible to recall to mind the peculiar atmosphere of the dream and to communicate it to another person. As the Swiss poet Carl Spitteler (a contemporary of Nietzsche's) said, "Dreams cannot be told; they dissolve when the rational mind tries to grasp them in words."[2]

What is a normal dream like? What does the ordinary "man on the street" dream about? Nietzsche was wrong when he wrote, "Either we have no dreams, or our dreams are interesting."[3] In most cases dreams are banal and uninteresting. Extensive studies made by the American researchers Hall, Van de Castle, and Snyder support this conclusion. Hall analyzed the reports of 1,000 people about their dreams at home; Snyder studied the reports of 650 people who were awakened from REM sleep in a laboratory. Evaluations of this considerable amount of dream material showed that only a small percentage of the dreams contained the bizarre and fantastic elements that we usually associate with them. It is clearly such untypical dreams that stick in our memory, while we forget the ordinary ones. The same studies produced other interesting results: it could be established that at least one other familiar person appears in almost all dreams. In approximately one-third of all dreams these persons or the dreamer himself are active in some way, either speaking to, listening to, or looking at something; in another third the persons in the dream are moving, either walking or riding in some form of vehicle. Physical activity does not seem to be hard work, as in waking life, but is accomplished easily and effortlessly. Another contrast to waking life is that routine activities like housework (cleaning or mending) and office tasks (for example, typing) rarely take place. The content of dreams tends to be more negative than positive. Unhappiness, defeat, and failure occur more often than contentment and success, and hostile and aggressive encounters are more frequent than friendly contact. But even if dreams contain very exciting events, the feelings accompanying them are strikingly subdued, and their intensity does not correspond in the least to the drama of the situation. Nevertheless, more than one-third of the dream reports contain feelings of fear and anxiety, although happier emotions are less common.

Children wake up from nightmares now and again and have difficulty going back to sleep. As we have already seen, they spend more time in REM sleep than adults. What do children dream about? This interesting but complex question was examined by David Foulkes, an American specializing in research on sleep and dreams, who made a systematic collection and investigation of the dreams of children in different age groups. It is especially difficult to get reliable accounts of dreams from small children. One of the problems is that the interviewer is not always able to tell whether the child knows how to distinguish dreams from waking experiences. Furthermore, the general difficulty of putting a dream into words is compounded by a small child's limited vocabulary.

The youngest group studied by Foulkes consisted of children between the ages of three and four. As a rule these children were capable of giving only short accounts of their dreams, which contained little action and emotion. They often dreamed about playing in familiar surroundings and about animals. The group of five- to six-year-olds was able to produce accounts twice as long as those of the younger children. They reported more movement and activity in their dreams; the people who appeared in them were for the most part family members and friends. The dreamers themselves played a strikingly passive role, however. An interesting phenomenon among this age group was that boys and girls tended to have different kinds of dreams: girls dreamed more often of friendly encounters, pleasant feelings, and "happy endings," whereas the boys' dreams dealt more with unhappy themes and conflicts. These differences were no longer identifiable among seven- and eight-year-old children.

In comparison with the younger age group, first- and second-graders played an active leading role more often in their dreams. The dreams of nine- to twelve-year-olds (preadolescents) generally took place at home, outdoors, or at school. The people appearing in them were family members or playmates, except that boys frequently dreamed about strangers of the male sex. Pleasant feelings were present more often than in younger groups. Older boys had aggressive dreams twice as often as girls. Among adolescents (thirteen- to fifteen-year-olds), especially among boys, pleasant dreams decreased and bizarre elements increased in frequency. Family members appeared less often.

The general conclusion to be drawn from these investigations is that, contrary to widespread assumptions, the majority of children's dreams are not disturbing or frightening. As children grow from toddlers to adolescents, the changes in their dreams reflect stages of cognitive development against a background of real-life situations: home environment, school, and the development of a personal and sexual identity.

Does "Dream Sleep" Exist?

Until REM sleep was discovered, studies of dreams could be conducted only by asking people to report their dreams after they had awakened in the morning. When it was learned that a large portion of REM sleep episodes is spent dreaming, experimental dream research received a tremendous impetus. An esoteric subject, which up until then had been the domain of a few specialists, was transformed—overnight, so to speak. It became a new field of research, one which could be investigated with scientific methods. This development benefited above all from the new possibility of obtaining accounts of dreams immediately following the dreaming process. To the surprise of many people who were convinced that they never dreamed at all or only very rarely, it could be shown that everyone dreams several times every night. Questions that had previously led to heated controversy, such as how long dreams last, could now be resolved by experiments.

In the older literature on dreams, one often comes across the hypothesis that even a long dream actually occurs within a few fractions of a second. Certain dream reports seem to bear this out, such as the following account of a dream of the nineteenth-century French psychologist Maury, as reported by Sigmund Freud:

He was ill and lying in his room in bed, with his mother sitting beside him, and dreamt that it was during the Reign of Terror. After witnessing a number of frightful scenes of murder, he was finally himself brought before the revolutionary tribunal. There he saw Robespierre, Marat, Fouquier-Tinville and the rest of the grim heroes of those terrible days. He was questioned by them, and, after a number of incidents which were not retained in his memory, was condemned, and led to the place of execution surrounded by an immense mob. He climbed onto the scaffold and was bound to the plank by the executioner. It was tipped up. The blade of the guillotine fell. He felt his head being separated from his body, woke up in extreme anxiety—and found that the top of the bed had fallen down and had struck his cervical vertebrae just in the way in which the blade of the guillotine would actually have struck them.[4]

This account suggests that an external event—the collapse of part of the bed in which Maury was sleeping—had prompted his dream, which would then have to have taken place within fractions of a second, and backward in time, so to speak—that is, with the end determining the beginning.

A few years after the discovery of REM sleep, Dement and his colleagues set about investigating the actual length of dreams. Sometimes they awakened subjects just after the start of REM sleep; at other times they allowed them a longer period of REM sleep before waking them up. The results showed that the length of the dreams reported corresponded to the length of REM sleep. Those people awakened early had had short dreams; those allowed to sleep longer, long ones. After very long REM sleep episodes (thirty to fifty minutes), the subjects had the feeling that they had been dreaming an unusually long time, but the accounts they could give of their dreams were no longer than when they were awakened fifteen minutes into a REM sleep period. Clearly, dreams begin to fade from memory even during the course of a long REM sleep episode. In other experiments Dement and Wolpert sprayed sleeping subjects with water, in order to mark a certain point in the passage of dreaming time. A portion of the subjects did in fact incorporate this sensory stimulation into their dreams. For example, a subject who had dreamed he was acting in a play related the following narrative when he was awakened thirty seconds after the cold water had been sprayed on his back:

> I was walking behind the leading lady when she suddenly collapsed and water was dripping on her. I ran over to her and water was dripping on my back and head. The roof was leaking. I was very puzzled why she fell down and decided some plaster must have fallen on her. I looked up and there was a hole in the roof. I dragged her over to the side of the stage and began pulling the curtains. Just then I woke up.[5]

The experimenters compared the length of time elapsed between the stimulation and waking of subjects with the length of the reported dreams. Once again the results indicated that the events of a dream corresponded approximately to the actual passage of time.

Another question that arose was whether the dreaming process manifests itself in any measurable body functions. Do the rapid eye movements of REM sleep, for instance, have any connection with the content of a dream? Dement's first results seemed to confirm this theory. He described an experiment in which a subject was awakened after a long sequence of eye movements, which had consisted of regular back-and-forth shifts from one direction to another. The sleeper reported that he had been dreaming about watching a long volley in a Ping-Pong game. But other experiments revealed no such connection between eye movements and dream content. It now seems quite unlikely that these two phenomena are directly related. Infants and animals also have rapid eye movements when they are asleep, and such movements more probably represent one of the "phasic processes" accompanying REM sleep. Other such phase-related phenomena are sudden jerks of the fingers and changes in blood pressure. It is still not possible today to draw any conclusions about what is taking place in a person's dream by measuring his body functions.

Freud tells us that dreamless sleep is the best kind of sleep —in fact, the only good kind. But can we really discriminate between "dreamless sleep" and "dream sleep"? Sleep researchers occasionally refer to REM sleep loosely as "dream sleep," since dreams are reported in 80 percent of the cases when subjects are awakened from this stage. Experiments have shown, however, that considering only REM sleep as dream sleep is an oversimplification, since the waking up of subjects from non-REM sleep also produces dream reports in up to 74 percent of the cases.

It can be said that dreams in these two stages of sleep tend to be dissimilar: accounts of dreams from REM sleep are in general livelier, more complex, bizarre, and more highly emotionally colored than dreams from non-REM sleep, in which rational and realistic elements similar to waking thoughts tend to prevail. Researchers who were not informed about the stages of sleep from which dream reports were obtained were able to distinguish dreams from REM and non-REM sleep solely on the basis of their content. However, John Antrobus, the American researcher on sleep and dreams, holds that the main difference between dreams in the two stages lies in their length, not in their content. In his opinion the longer dreams typical of REM sleep offer more opportunity for colorful elements than the short, non-REM dreams. These differences in length could arise from the fact that memory is better after a person is awakened from REM sleep than after awakening from non-REM sleep.

The relationship between dreams and sleep stages contains a further interesting aspect: experiences similar to dreams occur not only when we are asleep at night but also as we are falling asleep or waking up. In his diary the Austrian writer Robert Musil described the peculiar sensation of drifting back and forth between the worlds of thinking and dreaming that we can have if we wake up slowly:

> Dream thoughts. Observed them in myself again early this morning. Most of it forgotten, unfortunately. It is half-dreamed, half-thought. Dreamed, but not without my will being somehow in control, as it is during the day.
> It was something about nicotine. I had woken up, and some physical sensation had made me start thinking about wanting to smoke less for a day. Then drifted back half-asleep again; and then, suddenly, had a clear head again; apparently the urge to fix something firmly in my mind had woken me up. It was a terrible word for the effects of nicotine; now, hours later, all I can remember is an image of a model of the human body, made of wire or string, as in geometry class; its brain

seemed to be saturated, and there was a word for it, a word with a ghastly forcefulness.

I think even the first memory was no different; all I caught was the tail or the wake of it, as I so often do.[6]

Two American researchers, Gerald Vogel and David Foulkes, have made a detailed study of changes in the mental state of people falling asleep. Different phases can be distinguished. The first step is a loss of control over the flow of our thoughts. When we are awake, we think about one thing or another, steering our thoughts in the desired direction. As we fall asleep, our thoughts begin to wander and go their own way. If the subject of an experiment is awakened late in the phase of falling asleep, it can be observed that he has lost his orientation in time and space. He is no longer aware that he is lying in his bed at eleven o'clock at night. When the process of falling asleep has moved to a still later phase, the first actual dream images occur, and the sleeper no longer realizes that they do not correspond to external reality. Accounts of dreams from this phase of falling asleep resemble those from REM sleep so closely that it is not possible to tell them apart.

The experience of dreaming is thus by no means limited to REM sleep but also occurs as we fall asleep, wake up, and are in non-REM sleep. And so why not go one step further and ask whether mental processes resembling dreams are not also possible in a waking state? If we sit or lie down during the day, closing our eyes and relaxing, our thoughts begin to wander as well. We can become so engrossed in our fantasies that we lose the awareness of where we are. Indications actually exist that daydreams and nighttime dreams are similar in character and in content. The states of dreaming and of waking consciousness appear not to be fundamentally different from one another. We can experience a kind of "inward turning" of our thoughts and mental images during waking periods that resembles dreaming. This state of mind can favor the creative or artistic imagination.

Let us conclude this section with a few words about night-mares. They are dream experiences of a frightening nature, occurring usually in the second half of the night, in a REM sleep stage, and ending with our waking up with a start. We can remember the dream but are aware that it was only a dream. The occurrence of so-called *pavor nocturnus* (night terrors) is a different matter. Here the dreamer wakes up screaming and still frightened; he is covered with perspiration and is breathing rapidly. Even after waking up, he remains disoriented and cannot give any account of the dream. Children may need five to ten minutes before they recover and calm down. The memory of this incident has completely vanished by the next morning. These two types of anxiety dreams reflect the characteristic differences between an awakening from REM sleep and an awakening from the deep-sleep stage of non-REM sleep. A person awakened from a REM sleep episode is immediately oriented and aware of his surroundings, whereas one awakened from deep sleep experiences a period of extreme drowsiness, disorientation, and limited memory function.

Dreams—Sense or Nonsense?

Are dreams merely illusions, or do they reveal significant associations of ideas? Ever since philosophers began to reflect on this question, there have been believers in both camps. One can imagine Sigmund Freud writing the following sentence taken from Plato's *Republic:* ". . . in fact there exists in every one of us, even in some reputed most respectable, a terrible, fierce, and lawless brood of desires, which it seems are revealed in our sleep."[7] Aristotle, however, saw in dreams merely the remnants of sensory impressions, accidental like "the eddies often seen in rivers . . . often with unchanging pattern, but often again dividing into other shapes owing to some obstruction."[8]

In this passage Aristotle offers a theory to explain the origin of dreams that was held in high favor by the positivists of the nineteenth century. The scientific school of psychology of the last century had very little interest in the study of dreams. The German scientist and philosopher Fechner wrote disparagingly that it was "as though [in dreams] psychological activity had been transported from the brain of a reasonable man into that of a fool."[9] Dreams were viewed as the aftereffects of sensory impressions received during waking hours and as the results of changes in body position during sleep. The bizarre quality of dream images was traced to a reduction in the quality of mental activity in sleep; this manifested itself, according to Maury, in a "whole range of degradations of intellectual and rational capacities."[10] It must be said that such considerations led to concrete experiments, in which the influence of sensory stimuli on dreams was investigated, but interpretations of the results were often inadequate. It is amusing to read today Freud's account of Maury's findings:

1. His lips and the tip of his nose were tickled with a feather.—He dreamt of a frightful form of torture.
2. A pair of scissors was sharpened on a pair of pliers.—He heard bells pealing, followed by alarm-bells, and he was back in the June days of 1848. . . .
8. A drop of water was dropped on his forehead.—He was in Italy, was sweating violently and was drinking white Orvieto wine.[11]

In the last few years scientists have drawn on new developments in neurophysiology to explain dreams. According to one new hypothesis, external sensory stimuli do not play the major role; rather, the dream state is generated by the activity of the brain itself. Two American psychiatrists who pursue research on sleep, Robert McCarley and Allan Hobson, suggested that dream images and their abrupt shifts during REM sleep are caused by an activation of the neural networks associated with vision and eye movement. According to their view, impressions of motion in dreams arise from excitation of the motor regions of the brain, whereas emotional components and memories of the past are related to other regions of the forebrain. The bizarre nature of dream experiences comes about from simultaneous activation of different cerebral systems, so that the brain receives contradictory information. Dreams as a whole are considered to represent a synthesis of these various elements. Unfortunately it is difficult to test this hypothesis in experiments; in addition, the theory is designed to explain only dreams from REM sleep. Such neurobiological theories typically regard dreams as basically meaningless epiphenomena of neural activity. All that dream analysis can do, they would say, is to provide information about how the brain functions.

Even earlier authors attempted to explain the origin of dreams in terms of physical processes. For example, the German philosopher Immanuel Kant credited dreams with a meaningful biological function, seeing in them a "regulation of nature" that had not only some purpose but possibly even a "curative" effect:

Now, in just the same way, I would ask if dreams (from which our sleep is never free, although we rarely remember what we have dreamed), may not be a regulation of nature adapted to ends. For when all the muscular forces of the body are relaxed dreams serve the purpose of internally stimulating the vital organs by means of the imagination and the great activity which it exerts—an activity that in this state generally rises to psycho-physical agitation. This seems to be why imagination is usually more actively at work in the sleep of those who have gone to bed at night with a loaded stomach, just when this stimulation is most needed. Hence, I would suggest that without this internal stimulating force and fatiguing unrest that makes us complain of our dreams, which in fact, however, are probably curative, sleep, even in a sound state of health, would amount to a complete extinction of life.[12]

But let us return to the present day. The husband-and-wife research team of Dietrich Lehmann and Marta Koukkou at the University of Zurich has proposed a theoretical model of dreams that suggests that in our sleep we combine ideas and strategies of thinking originating in childhood with recently acquired relevant information. Dreams are considered to be the result of the restructuring and reinterpretation of the data stored in memory. In the authors' view, therefore, dreams represent not accidental but meaningful occurrences. This dream theory bears a certain resemblance to Jouvet's hypothesis that in REM sleep genetically determined information (i.e., inborn, instinctual behavior) is related to recently acquired information (sensory information, learned behavior). We shall return to this hypothesis, which is concerned mainly with REM sleep and not with dreams, in chapter 12.

Very recently the molecular biologists Francis Crick and Graeme Mitchison presented yet another hypothesis to explain the origin of dreams in REM sleep. They suggested that REM dreams reflect the operation of a "cleaning-up mechanism" in the brain, which removes "parasitic" modes of behavior and excitations left over from our waking hours. "We dream in order to forget," the authors write. They call this process "reverse learning" or "unlearning," by which they mean the elimination of useless information from the brain. Their theory once again treats dreams as a biologically useful process, one that keeps the central nervous system functioning efficiently; however, the content of dreams, as they see it, is an accidental result that does not lend itself to meaningful interpretation. Like the other theories already mentioned, this hypothesis is difficult to confirm or disprove in experiments.

If we could assume that dreams serve a basic biological purpose, we would be justified in concluding that dreaming is an essential and indispensable process. The pre-Freudian psychologist Robert held just such a view:

> A man deprived of the capacity for dreaming would in course of time become mentally deranged, because a great mass of uncompleted, unworked-out thoughts and superficial impressions would accumulate in his brain and would be bound by their bulk to smother the thoughts which should be assimilated into memory as completed wholes.[13]

When Dement reported in 1960 that depriving subjects of REM sleep led to mental disturbances, medical and scientific professionals accepted his findings without surprise. His study was seen merely as confirmation of what had already been assumed to be true for a long time. The connection between REM sleep and mental health made such obvious sense, in fact, that refutations were simply not accepted, even when several careful follow-up studies failed to confirm the first results and Dement himself retracted his earlier statements. Thus textbooks today still contain passages about the devastating effects of "dream sleep deprivation." Such a view is scientifically unfounded, however, among other reasons because it has been established in the meantime that dreams occur in all stages of sleep. It is not possible to deprive a person of dreams altogether without depriving him of sleep altogether. Final answers to questions about the biological meaning of dreams, and whether they are necessary for health, cannot be given for the time being.

The Cultural Significance of Dreams

Let us now consider dreams in a broader historical and cultural context. The nineteenth-century German dramatist Friedrich Hebbel wrote, "Dreams are the best proof of the fact that we are not as securely locked inside our skins as it seems."[14] Since ancient times people have seen dreams as the gateway to another world. In the *Iliad* and *Odyssey* of Homer, the gods take on human form in dreams, in order to give mortals a task to perform, or to warn them of danger. The goddess Athena appears to the sleeping Nausicaa in the form of her best friend and tells her to go down to the beach at daybreak to wash clothes; in this way the shipwrecked Ulysses is rescued.

Dreams also had great importance for the practice of medicine in ancient Greece:

> In Greece there were dream oracles, which were regularly visited by patients in search of recovery. A sick man would enter the temple of Apollo or Aesculapius, would perform various ceremonies there, would be purified by lustration, massage and incense, and then, in a state of exaltation, would be stretched on the skin of a ram that had been sacrificed. He would then fall asleep and would dream of the remedies for his illness. These would be revealed to him either in their natural form or in symbols and pictures which would afterwards be interpreted by the priests.[15]

We also know that the ancient Egyptians paid great attention to dreams and ascribed very specific meanings to them. A papyrus from this era contains the following interpretations of dreams:

> If a woman kisses her husband, she will have trouble; . . .
> If an ass couples with her, she will be punished for a great fault;
> If a he-goat couples with her, she will die promptly; . . .
> If she gives birth to a cat, she will have many children;
> If she gives birth to a dog, she will have a boy.[16]

One of the most famous books on dreams was written by Artemidorus in the second century A.D. Numerous later books of a similar kind were based on this work. Artemidorus gives direct translations for dream symbols. A foot appearing in a dream, for example, means a slave; a head means a father. Some symbols had prophetic significance: a dolphin in water is a good omen; a dolphin on land, a bad one.

Many different cultures share the belief that through dreams contact with another form of reality becomes possible. In the Vedic texts of ancient India, dreams were regarded as an intermediate stage between this world and the next. It was thought that the soul leaves the body during sleep, carried and protected by the sleeper's breath, and floats in space, where it can survey both worlds. Not until modern times did dreams come to be viewed in a fundamentally different manner, namely, that this "other" reality is not a region outside the body but instead a part of the dreamer's own mind. If dreams represent not an inspiration or revelation from another world, however, but a product of our own selves, then the question arises whether we must bear the responsibility for them. The pre-Freudian psychologist Haffner firmly rejected such a conclusion:

> We are not responsible for our dreams, since our thought and will have been deprived in them of the basis upon which alone our life possesses truth and reality. . . . For that reason no dream-wishes or dream-actions can be virtuous or sinful.[17]

Nietzsche contradicted this view with biting contempt:

> You would wish to be responsible for everything except your dreams! What miserable weakness, what lack of logical courage! Nothing contains more of your own work than your dreams! Nothing belongs to you so much! Substance, form, duration, actor, spectator—in these comedies you act as your complete selves![18]

Freud outlined this set of problems with his usual clarity and brilliant simplicity:

Our scientific consideration of dreams starts off from the assumption that they are products of our own mental activity. Nevertheless the finished dream strikes us as something alien to us. We are so little obliged to acknowledge our responsibility for it that [in German] we are just as ready to say *"mir hat geträumt"* ["I had a dream," literally "a dream came to me"] as *"ich habe geträumt"* ["I dreamt"]. What is the origin of this feeling that dreams are extraneous to our minds?[19]

Freud presented an answer to this question in his epoch-making work *The Interpretation of Dreams.* There he stated that dreams contain not only an obvious, "manifest" meaning that can be summed up in their retelling but also a hidden, "latent" meaning not immediately recognizable or intelligible. To understand this second aspect, an interpreter would need further information about the person who had the dream. Vogel and Foulkes demonstrate the importance of these ideas of Freud's nicely in the following example:

A man who is a subject in a sleep laboratory experiment reports the following dream: "I am riding a bicycle." Imagine that we, the researchers, want to find the experiential sources of this dream, its mode of construction, its meaning and its function. We use the methods commonly employed in dream research for the past twenty years: the dream is rated and content analyzed according to criteria which do not require information as to who dreamed the dream or when. Using these criteria, we note that the dream has a relatively realistic or plausible theme and that it contains only the dreamer, who is an actively participating character manifesting no affect as he performs gross locomotor activity in connection with a vehicular object. We note no aggressive or sexual themes, and conclude that it is rather prosaic in quality, seeming not to touch on any deep concerns of the dreamer's life. . . .

Suppose, however, that instead of using approaches which depend on publicly observable knowledge of the manifest dream, we ask the subject what comes to his mind about bicycles. In abbreviated form, his reply is this: "Bicycling brings two things to mind. First, it is my son's hobby and he is going away to college in the fall. I want to spend more time with him and share with him some of the things he likes to do before he goes off to make his own way in life. The second, darker association is that my father died less than a year ago of heart disease. He was an exerciser—he had a stationary bicycle. I think I need to exercise more strenuously to avoid his fate."[20]

The chain of associations revealed that this dream was not merely an insignificant episode that happened to involve a bicycle; instead, it was closely connected with the two most important male figures in the dreamer's life. But such a meaning, hidden at first, can be uncovered only when the manifest content is analyzed in the wider context of a person's experiences.

It is beyond doubt one of Freud's great achievements to have pointed out, emphatically and convincingly, this deeper level of meaning. Dreams are not merely shadows, as Hamlet says, but rather "letters to oneself." They employ a metaphorical language with rules different from those of ordinary speech. Each element of a dream is linked with a multitude of other thoughts and ideas. The connections between them can be brought to light in various ways; one of the most important is the technique known as free association, in which subjects should allow their thoughts to wander as freely as possible, and recount candidly what occurs to them in connection with single elements. The process underlying the dream, called "dream work" by Freud, begins by interweaving and condensing very disparate ideas and impressions into a single dream image. In addition to condensing, dreams also work by "displacing" thoughts, that is, putting them in a different and seemingly meaningless context. Freud held that such a process served to disguise sensitive topics, when they are too emotionally loaded to be "admitted" into dreams.

This is not the place to go into the detailed mechanisms of dream work. However, it is important to recall that Freud understood dreams as a special and meaningful language of the mind. David Foulkes developed this approach further in his book *A Grammar of Dreams.* Starting with Freud's doctrines, but incorporating results from modern psychological and linguistic research, Foulkes developed a method for uncovering the hidden, latent structures within the manifest content of dreams. In addition to the straightforward account of a dream, the dreamer's free associations play an important role. Foulkes created a model based on mathematical concepts to describe the transformation processes.

"The world of dreams is not less real than the world of waking; it is just real in a different way."[21] One might agree with Ludwig Klages's conclusion that the analysis of dreams gives us deeper insights into the mind's functions. Can the results of such research be of any use to nonspecialists? Dreams play a role in many forms of psychotherapy, which seek in them a way of gaining access to currents deep in the mind. One of Freud's best-known sayings is that "the interpretation of dreams is in fact the royal road to a knowledge of the unconscious."[22]

We shall leave this royal road here, however, to mention other indications that dreams can be useful for the activities of our waking hours. "Creative" dreams suggest just this, as in the famous account of the German chemist Friedrich August Kekulé, who had long been searching without success for the chemical structure of benzene. One night he dreamed about six snakes, which were biting each other's tails and formed a large revolving circle. When he woke up, he had the solution to his problem: the structure of benzene resembles the ring of six snakes and consists of a closed ring of six carbon atoms.

Although such creative achievements are hardly the rule in dreams, a popular saying recommends that the best way to deal with a difficult problem is to "sleep on it." Perhaps this piece of folk wisdom refers to the creative aspect of our dream life, in which thoughts rove more freely. Looser associations can let us find solutions that we seek in vain in our conscious, waking hours.

The desire to harness and make use of the power of dreams has led some people to attempt to master the art of "lucid dreaming." In contrast to normal sleepers, the lucid dreamer can maintain his awareness that he is dreaming. This awareness, in turn, is supposed to liberate his mind from the dream's control and allow him to move freely in his "dream landscape." Accounts of such lucid dreams have been frequently reported, but it has not yet been possible to confirm them scientifically.

In the book *Journey to Ixtlan,* by Carlos Castaneda, the Mexican magician Don Juan gives his pupil instructions for a first dream exercise. Before falling asleep, he should concentrate on looking at his hands in his dream and make himself aware that he is dreaming. As the dream continues, he should shift his gaze from his hands to another object and then bring his eyes back to rest on his hands again.

> Every time you look at anything in your dream it changes shape. . . . The trick in learning to *set up dreaming* is obviously not just to look at things but to sustain the sight of them. *Dreaming* is real, when one has succeeded in bringing everything into focus. Then there is no difference between what you do when you sleep and what you do when you are not sleeping.[23]

After these elementary exercises, Don Juan teaches his pupil to choose a place to travel to in his dream. Few people besides Don Juan can claim to have acquired this ability, but it is nevertheless fascinating to think that the world of dreams, which normally eludes the grasp of our reason, could be brought under conscious control.

Let us end this discussion about the meaning of dreams with an excursion into the field of anthropology. The Senoi were a peaceful people who still existed in the remote jungles of

Malaysia at the beginning of this century. They attached great importance to dreams, since they regarded them as a mirror not only of existing currents in their lives but also of feelings just beginning to develop. If someone dreamed about quarreling with his best friend, this was interpreted to mean an unconscious conflict, even if no sign of it could yet be seen in daily life. The appropriate reaction to such a dream was to discuss its contents within the dreamer's own family, and also with the friend in question; the dreamer then gave this friend a present, in order to remove the unconscious clouding of the relationship. In such a situation the dreamer would strive to follow his first dream with a lucid one, in which he could meet the dream image of his friend and assure him of his friendship. The Senoi taught their children to treat threatening dream images as problematical parts of their own selves; they encouraged the children to have the nightmare again, either to conquer the threatening figure, to make friends with it, or—a third possibility— to be conquered by it and to end the conflict in this way. The ethnologist Stewart describes the Senoi as a thoroughly civilized people, who managed, to a great extent, to live without mental illnesses and warlike conflicts. Unfortunately the culture of the Senoi disappeared almost completely in the upheavals of the Second World War.

Perhaps the German poet Friedrich Hölderlin had in mind similar ideas about the possibilities of dreams when he wrote, "Men are kings—when they dream, and beggars when they reason."[24]

5

Sleep and Sleeping Pills

. . . not poppy, nor mandragora,
Nor all the drowsy syrups of the world,
Shall ever medicine thee to that sweet sleep
Which thou owedst yesterday.
—WILLIAM SHAKESPEARE
Othello

Sleeping pills are taken more often than almost any other kind of drug. In the United States, for instance, six to nine million adults each year take some form of medication in order to sleep. Almost 40 percent of them are aged sixty and older, although this age group makes up only 15 percent of the population as a whole. The consumption of sleeping pills thus rises dramatically with increasing age. How do these widely used medicines work? What are their advantages, and what risks do they entail? And a further, very important question: Do these drugs really produce a natural form of sleep?

Sleeping pills as such have existed only for the last hundred years or so. Of course, many attempts have been made earlier to induce sleep with elixirs and herbal mixtures, for the problem of insomnia is as old as human history. In the Middle Ages physicians applied salves, sponges, poultices, and compresses to treat sleep disorders as well as to anesthetize patients before operations. Alcohol has been known as an easily available sleeping aid since ancient times, but, as we shall see, it usually produces only a brief period of inebriated and not very refresh-

ing sleep, followed by the disagreeable symptoms of a hangover. Opium, hashish, and derivatives of the nightshade family
of plants (e.g., belladonna) were also often prescribed in former
times for people who could not sleep. We know today, however, that all these substances employed in the days before
scientific pharmacology were not very effective. The first "real"
hypnotics (sleep-inducing medicines) were chloral hydrate and
paraldehyde, which came into use in the last twenty years of
the nineteenth century. They still figure among modern-day
medicines, but their unpleasant taste and smell tend to limit
their use.

Barbiturates: The "Classic" Sleeping Pills of an Earlier Era

Barbituric acid was discovered in 1864 by Adolf von Baeyer, a
twenty-nine-year-old research assistant, who synthesized it
from malonic acid and urea. This successful synthesis—so runs
the story—was celebrated in the city of Ghent, in Belgium, at
a tavern popular with the officers of an artillery regiment. Since
it happened to be the anniversary of their patron saint, St.
Barbara, the new substance was called barbiturate. According
to other, equally unconfirmed reports, a lady called Barbara
played a role in the selection of the chemical's name.

Barbiturates were introduced in medicine in the form of
sleeping pills at the beginning of this century and soon became
immensely popular. Of the more than 2,500 barbiturate compounds that have been synthesized, about fifty found medicinal
uses. Throughout the first half of the twentieth century, barbiturates were by far the most frequently prescribed drugs for
the treatment of sleep disorders, but although they had shown
themselves to be reliable and effective, their use went hand in
hand with certain disadvantages and risks. A tenfold overdose
is sufficient to cause serious poisoning, which first manifests

itself as confusion and then may lead to unconsciousness. The regulation of breathing and circulation are partially impaired. A condition of shock, accompanied by lung and kidney failure, and hypothermia (subnormal body temperature) represent further serious complications. A person suffering from an overdose of barbiturates must be treated quickly if he is to have a good chance of recovery. Another disadvantage of barbiturates is that negligence can cause accidental poisonings in children. On the other hand, an overdose of barbiturates frequently has been ingested to commit suicide. As late as 1963 some 10 percent of all suicides in the United States were committed by this means. As these medicines ceased to be used so widely, the number of suicides caused by barbiturates declined markedly.

Like other sleeping pills, barbiturates can lead to addiction. Occasionally people take these substances in combination with opiates, in order to intensify the resulting "high." If the drug is suddenly discontinued, a barbiturate addict may experience serious and even life-threatening withdrawal symptoms.

Efforts to develop sleeping pills without the disadvantages and risks of barbiturates began many years ago. In 1956 it finally seemed that a breakthrough had been achieved: the highly effective drug Thalidomide was marketed and quickly gained popularity. Its great advantage over barbiturates was that even large overdoses produced no symptoms of poisoning, and so it looked as if a "safe" sleeping pill had been found at last. Five full years had to pass before the medical world realized that one of the worst catastrophes in the history of pharmacology had occurred. Women who had taken the drug during pregnancy gave birth to horribly deformed babies, some of whom were missing arms and legs. It is estimated that about ten thousand such children were born and that about half of them survived. Since this disaster, laws requiring stringent testing of new drugs have been passed. Physicians now advise women in the early months of pregnancy to avoid not only sleeping pills but also other kinds of medication, if there are no compelling reasons for their use.

Modern Sleeping Pills: Benzodiazepines

Today drugs known to physicians and pharmacists as benzodiazepines occupy the prominent position that barbiturates held for fifty years. About one hundred million prescriptions for drugs of the benzodiazepine class are written in the United States every year. This new class of drugs was introduced in the early sixties, as tranquilizers to begin with—the best-known brand names were Librium and Valium—and their use spread rapidly throughout the world. Several years passed before it was realized that the tranquilizing effect of benzodiazepines could also be employed to induce sleep. The following table contains a list of typical benzodiazepine sleeping pills, but drugs of the tranquilizer type, which cannot be sharply distinguished from sleeping pills, are sometimes prescribed for sleep disorders as well.

The introduction of benzodiazepines represented considerable progress with respect to barbiturates and other "classical" hypnotics. Although an overdose of benzodiazepine may lead to poisoning and their chronic use to addiction, these risks are less severe than with the older drugs. An overdose of benzodiazepines alone rarely causes death. However, it must be emphasized that they can be dangerous when they are taken in high doses together with alcohol or other psychoactive drugs (i.e., those that affect mood or alter the state of consciousness). Benzodiazepines are effective sleep-inducing medicines that can be administered in doses ten to one hundred times smaller than those required for the "classic" barbiturates. Table 5.1 lists commonly used hypnotics and indicates how fast they are eliminated from the body. The "elimination half-life" can be defined, in a simplified way, as the amount of time it takes for the drug to decline to 50 percent of its original level in the body. Although other factors are equally important (for example, the rate of absorption in the intestines and the extent of distribution throughout the body), the elimination half-life is an im-

TABLE 5.1
Sleeping Pills of the Benzodiazepine Type

International Name	Brand Name (in the USA) if available	Half-Life
Flurazepam	Dalmane	3 days
Flunitrazepam		1 day
Nitrazepam		1 day
Lormetazepam		½ day
Temazepam	Restoril	½ day
Triazolam	Halcion	2–3 hours
Midazolam		2–3 hours

Note: "half-life" indicates the elimination half-life of a medicine or of its active metabolite.

portant indication of how long a drug remains in the organism. The table shows that the first three medicines have a long half-life. As Flurazepam is broken down within the body, it is transformed into another substance that also has a soporific effect and a half-life of several days. If Flurazepam is taken on several consecutive evenings, its concentration in the blood rises gradually, so that after intake for seven to ten days its level in the body is four to six times higher than after a single night. This effect is known as "cumulation."

The Effectiveness of Sleeping Pills

Most sleeping pills available in pharmacies have been proven effective. In former times, the effectiveness of a drug was assessed entirely on the basis of reports from doctors and patients. Today, all new drugs undergo strict laboratory tests to document their effects and side-effects. This is necessary because we cannot assume that all medicines labeled sleeping pills actually contain an active pharmaceutical ingredient. It has long been known that certain patients with sleep disorders respond to placebos, that is, to pseudomedicines and pills containing no active ingredients. The suggestion that a sleeping pill will work, or the patient's expectation that he will sleep better, is sometimes enough to actually improve his sleep. Modern tests of new drugs must take the power of suggestion into account; they usually accomplish this by "double-blind" experiments, in which the effectiveness of the sleeping pill is compared with that of a placebo. The subjects of the experiment are given both the real drug and the placebo (which is identical in appearance) in a random sequence known neither to them nor to the experimenter. Who received the drug and on what night is revealed only after the experiment. A difference between the two treatments can with certainty be ascribed to the pharmacological action of the drug and not to a placebo effect.

Let us consider a specific example that illustrates the use of two common methods. Subjects of experiments or patients can either themselves evaluate the quality of their sleep, or their sleep can be recorded and measured. Figure 5.1 illustrates a hundred-millimeter "self-rating scale." After waking up in the morning, subjects are asked to report their sleep quality on three scales, which are labeled "undisturbed"–"disturbed," "deep"–"superficial," and "very refreshing–little refreshing." The marks in each scale indicate the direction in which the "drug"-sleep deviated from a normal night's sleep; a mark in the middle means no difference at all. The evaluation of the responses consists merely of measuring the section marked on the scale. Although it looks deceptively simple and inexact, this procedure has proved to be a very sensitive method for registering subjective changes in the quality of sleep, even after quite small doses of drugs.

Figure 5.2 depicts the results of a procedure that does not depend on subjective statements of the experimental subject. In this method, the subject wears a small device on his wrist that registers his movements over a whole night. This activity monitor records and stores the total number of movements over consecutive seven-and-a-half-minute intervals. The upper dia-

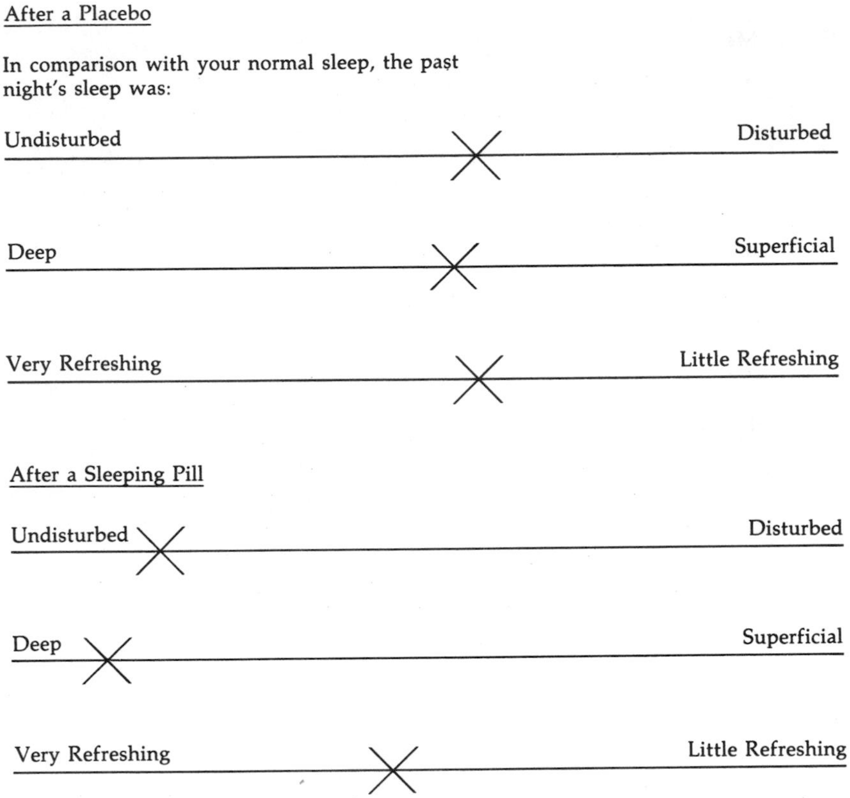

After a Placebo

In comparison with your normal sleep, the past
night's sleep was:

Undisturbed   ✕   Disturbed

Deep   ✕   Superficial

Very Refreshing   ✕   Little Refreshing

After a Sleeping Pill

Undisturbed ✕   Disturbed

Deep ✕   Superficial

Very Refreshing   ✕   Little Refreshing

FIGURE 5.1

Self-rating Scale After a Placebo and After a Sleeping Pill.
Those people who take a sleeping pill tend to assess their sleep the next
morning as having been deep and undisturbed. The ratings are made on
a self-rating scale, on which subjects compare their sleep after a sleeping
pill with their normal sleep by marking a cross. This simple procedure
produces accurate results for evaluating the effectiveness of different medications.

Without Medication

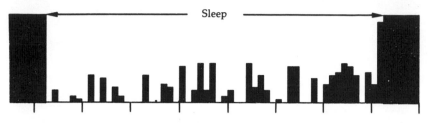

With a Sleeping Pill

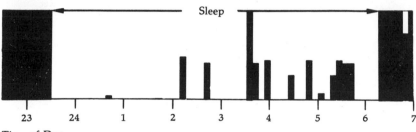

Time of Day

FIGURE 5.2
Movements During Sleep.
Sleeping pills reduce body movements in the night. In the upper diagram the number of movements of a good sleeper were recorded at seven-and-a-half-minute intervals. Such movements are normal and caused by changing position while asleep. The lower diagram shows the record of a subject who took a sleeping pill. The first few hours of sleep reflect a clear suppressive effect on body movements. The measurement of body movements is a sensitive and accurate method for testing the effectiveness of sleeping pills.

gram shows the record of a placebo night; after the subject has fallen asleep, periods of complete immobility alternate with periods of more or less activity. In the lower diagram (representing a night on which the subject took a benzodiazepine sleeping pill) the periods of immobility are significantly longer, particularly in the first half of the night. Drugs thus not only contribute to a subjective impression of better rest but also decrease the amount of objectively recordable movement during the night.

The most precise information about the effectiveness of sleeping pills can be obtained by polygraphic recordings in the sleep laboratory described in chapter 2. The quality of data obtained by this method is high, but so is the cost. The technique has two main advantages, however: we can discriminate exactly between sleeping and waking periods, and we can also investigate drug effects on the different stages of sleep. A really good sleeping pill scores high in three different categories: it shortens sleep latency (the amount of time elapsing between going to bed and falling asleep); it reduces the frequency and length of wake periods during the night; and it increases the total sleeping time. Sleeping pills may improve sleep primarily in the early or later part of the night, depending on whether the hypnotic effect of a drug has a rapid onset or persists for a long time.

How Do Sleeping Pills Affect Sleep Stages and the EEG?

The perfect sleeping pill would induce sleep that is indistinguishable from natural sleep. Unfortunately, this ideal medication exists only in the visions of physicians and pharmacists, since all the drugs in use today alter sleep stages and the sleep EEG. In the early 1960s the Scottish psychiatrist and researcher Ian Oswald observed that barbiturates reduce the total amount of REM sleep. In his experiment the percentage of REM sleep dropped from the normal 20–25 percent to 10–15 percent of sleep time. After the drug was discontinued, a "REM sleep rebound" occurred, as in the next few nights the subjects' REM sleep rose well above the normal values (i.e., up to 30–40 percent). The opinions prevailing about REM sleep in the early sixties have been mentioned in chapter 4; it was thought then that the occurrence of REM sleep is a prerequisite for the restorative or refreshing effects of sleep. This opinion, not confirmed by later experiments, led to a further conclusion: namely, that the suppression of REM sleep caused by most sleeping pills had especially negative consequences. Pharmaceutical companies in those days outdid each other in claiming that their product did not influence REM sleep at all or, at least, that it influenced it less than their competitors' pills did. Careful investigations soon showed that sleep-inducing drugs had a suppressive effect not only on REM sleep but on deep slow-wave sleep as well. This reduction of deep sleep was often observed, being especially noticeable after the administration of benzodiazepines. But unlike the case of REM sleep, the discontinuation of a benzodiazepine does not lead to a rebound of deep sleep; instead, there is a gradual return to the baseline level.

In my own laboratory, our research group has used the method of EEG spectral analysis described in chapter 2 in order to take a closer look at the effects of different benzodiazepines. Figure 5.3 shows the extent to which a single dose of such a drug can alter the EEG. The records are from an experiment in which a subject was given on two consecutive nights a placebo and a popular, effective benzodiazepine sleeping pill (flunitrazepam—2 milligrams). The recordings reveal that during the drug night the peaks of EEG slow-wave activity (in the range of 1–9 Hz) that correspond to deep sleep are greatly reduced. On the other hand, the peaks of the moderately rapid EEG frequencies (in the range of 9–14 Hz) are increased. Finally, we see that in the high-frequency range (14–25 Hz), peaks occur during REM sleep on the drug night that are not present during the placebo night. It is striking that these considerable differences between the two EEG recordings are barely reflected by the standard sleep profile (shown at the top of figure 5.3). The reason for this is that the conventional sleep stage criteria have been derived from changes occurring in drug-free, natural sleep. As a result, the abnormal EEG variations caused by a

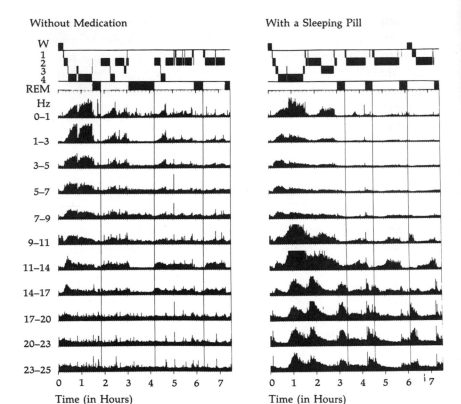

Without Medication   With a Sleeping Pill

Time (in Hours)   Time (in Hours)

FIGURE 5.3
The Stages of Sleep and EEG Spectra.

Sleeping pills alter the electrical activity of the brain during sleep. As in figure 2.6, the sleep profile is shown at the top of the diagram and the EEG spectrum below. Here the recordings of one subject's sleep on two different nights are illustrated. The left-hand diagram shows a normal night (without medication), while the right-hand one is from a night when a sleeping pill was taken. The medication suppresses slow-wave activity in the EEG and increases the activity in the range of intermediate and rapid waves. Abnormal activity in the rapid-wave range occurs during REM sleep. Spectral analysis allows us to recognize changes not visible in the sleep profile.

sleeping pill have only a limited effect on the sleep stages. The spectral analysis of the EEG is able to document such changes more faithfully. It is thus evident that modern sleeping pills also alter the EEG signs of natural sleep, although scientists are still not entirely sure how to interpret them. It is still unclear whether the drug-induced EEG changes indicate some impairment in brain function or in the restorative effects of sleep.

Aftereffects of Sleeping Pills

Ideally, sleeping pills ought to promote sleep during the night but have no influence on the organism during the following day. But this is frequently not the case. In my group, we recently conducted experiments to measure the aftereffects of several widely prescribed benzodiazepine hypnotics. We gave them to our subjects in capsule form before they went to sleep. In the case of one popular brand with a long half-life, ten out of twelve people complained of drowsiness, an aftereffect that persisted until about noontime. We showed for different compounds that alertness and performance were still impaired at 9 A.M. The subjects were asked to type a text consisting of a sequence of nonsense words, within twenty minutes and with as few errors as possible. If they had taken a sleeping pill the preceding night, they made more mistakes. Other test methods also confirmed that sleeping pills can impair performance on the next day. While such aftereffects are sometimes irrelevant, they can become important if the tasks to be performed require a high level of concentration and attention. Because of the continuing tranquilizing effects of such drugs, patients occasionally fail to recognize that they are less alert than normal, and so they overestimate their own capacities. In Finland, for example, tests showed that a relatively high percentage of drivers involved in car accidents had benzodiazepines in their blood. The aftereffects of benzodiazepines were registered not only on the next day but even during the following night. With the aid of EEG spectral analysis, we were recently able to demonstrate that the effect of a single dose of a sleep-inducing drug on the sleep EEG persisted during the following drug-free night.

A different kind of aftereffect was described for the first time a few years ago. It is called rebound insomnia and occurs when a rapidly eliminated sleeping pill is suddenly discontinued and as a consequence sleep is disturbed. It appears that the brain somehow adapts to a hypnotic that is used over a longer period of time; when the drug is discontinued, withdrawal symptoms appear, and for a few nights sleep becomes more disturbed and superficial. Unfortunately, when this happens, patients often return to the pills in order to get a good night's sleep, and thus are liable to become dependent. A gradual reduction of the dosage can help prevent the unpleasant aftereffect of rebound insomnia.

As people get older, they frequently have more trouble sleeping well, and so the consumption of sleeping pills increases among the elderly. But they often have problematical reactions to such drugs as well, and the aftereffects are more pronounced in their age group: dizziness, confusion, and memory loss can occur. Such symptoms may mistakenly be regarded as symptoms of senility. Particular caution in the use of sleeping pills is required for older people.

How Do Sleeping Pills Work?

It is often true in pharmacology that new drugs are discovered by accident; they rarely result from rational, scientific deductions. Sleeping pills are no exception. As a consequence, we can describe quite well the effects and side effects of the most common sleep-inducing drugs, but the truth of the matter is that we know hardly anything about the mechanisms that produce these effects. A recent discovery has raised hopes that we will soon know more about how sleeping pills work. In 1977 a Swiss and a Danish research team discovered that benzodiazepines are bound to specific sites of nerve-cell membranes (receptors). These findings were particularly exciting because a few years earlier the discovery of the binding mechanism of opiates (such as morphine and heroin) in the brain had led to the identification of endogenous opiates. Endogenous opiates are pain-relieving substances produced by the body itself; they are known as endorphins and enkephalins. It was not farfetched to think that there could also exist endogenous substances that are bound to benzodiazepine receptors and thus might function as natural tranquilizers or sleep inducers. In spite of the most intensive efforts, however, the search for such substances has so far been unsuccessful. Yet all this research activity has not been entirely in vain, since not long ago scientists were able to synthesize substances that occupy the benzodiazepine receptors but do not produce any measurable biological effect. These are known as benzodiazepine antagonists; when administered to patients, they rapidly counteract the effects of sleeping pills. Perhaps these new substances will some day make it possible to strictly limit the effects of benzodiazepine drugs to the nighttime. However, it is still too early to predict how these interesting new compounds will be applied in medicine.

"Natural" Medicines for Sleep Disorders

Up to now our discussion has been limited to drugs that require a doctor's prescription. However, natural substances to treat sleep problems and "over-the-counter" drugs also exist in large numbers. Herbal extracts, in particular, have been popular home remedies for a long time. In several European countries, preparations based on the valerian root are among the most widespread medicines of this type, but in spite of their popularity their effectiveness has rarely been studied in detail. Recently

Peter Leathwood, a researcher working in Switzerland, investigated whether a water-soluble extract of valerian influences sleep. In a double-blind experiment he studied 128 subjects, who before going to bed took capsules containing either the valerian extract or a placebo. The results based on questionnaires showed that the valerian capsules did in fact shorten sleep latency. The medication also improved the quality of sleep. The effects were most pronounced among the habitual poor sleepers. It would now be desirable to confirm these results in follow-up experiments and to study more closely the dose-effect relationship. It would also be important to isolate the active substances in the extract; in collaboration with Gisela Balderer, a research pharmacist, we are investigating these problems.

In the last few years there has been a lot of talk about L-tryptophan. It is an amino acid (a building block of proteins) that is contained in our normal diet at a daily level of 0.5–2.0 grams. Although some studies indicated that L-tryptophan has a hypnotic effect, other studies have not confirmed these claims. Given the currently available information, we must conclude that if this substance does promote sleep, its effects are weak at best. It has been claimed that a sleep-promoting effect occurred in patients with chronic sleep disturbances after repeated administration. We cannot exclude the fact that a subgroup of the population may respond to L-tryptophan. However, based on the available evidence, tryptophan does not appear to be a potent and reliable hypnotic.

Other front-runners among home remedies for insomnia are alcoholic drinks. Even though "hard" scientific data are lacking here as well, it is reasonable to assume that a nightcap does indeed make it easier for many people to fall asleep. The problem with alcohol is that small amounts have too weak an effect in cases of serious sleep disorders, while larger doses work better, but often only in the first part of the night. As figure 5.4 shows, rebound insomnia tends to occur toward morning, leaving the would-be sleeper awake in bed for a long time. The

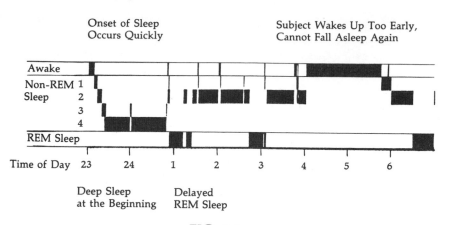

FIG. 5.4.

A Sleep Profile After Alcohol Intake.

Alcohol is a poor sleep aid. This sleep profile, made after the subject had drunk one-half liter (about one pint) of red wine, shows that the subject fell asleep quickly but did not remain asleep the whole night. Toward morning, between 4 and 6 A.M., the subject lay awake in bed for almost two hours. The onset of REM sleep is delayed. Undesirable aftereffects (hangover) are common on the following day.

American physician E. T. Hurd observed as early as 1891, "Unfortunately, the sleep produced by alcohol is often of short duration; the patient awakes after a couple of hours but little refreshed, and may be awake much of the night without being able to go to sleep again."[1] In addition, the symptoms of a hangover are the most familiar and least popular aftereffects of this drug.

Herbal preparations, long a part of folk medicine, are sometimes praised as "natural" remedies, and their use is often promoted by the idea that they produce a more natural sleep than medicines created artificially in a chemistry laboratory. These opinions are based more on wishful thinking than on well-founded scientific arguments. We should keep in mind when dealing with such questions that substances of plant origin do not necessarily produce only beneficial effects. They can also have dangerous side-effects, and various examples, such as the carcinogenic effect of nicotine in tobacco, are familiar enough. The documentation of how these herbal substances work should therefore be based on scientific investigations that are as rigorous as those required for synthetic drugs.

In Conclusion

Let us return to sleeping pills as such to conclude this subject. Their risks, side effects, and aftereffects have been presented here in considerable detail because they are frequently disregarded or neglected by the medical profession and by patients. We ought to remember when using them that sleeping pills are potent medicines that may influence the regulation of sleep and other functions of the brain. Thus they should not be taken casually, but only when it has been demonstrated that they are necessary. And in such cases it is important to keep the dose as small as possible, and to limit its use to the shortest possible time period. It has been shown that the effectiveness of hypnotics decreases with prolonged use. However, despite the need for such precautions and the existence of possible undesired side-effects, the introduction of benzodiazepines must be regarded as one of the major recent advances in medicine.

6

"I Didn't Sleep a Wink All Night":
Insomnia and Disorders of Sleeping and Waking

> There is a gulf fixed between those who can sleep and those who cannot. It is one of the great divisions of the human race.
>
> —IRIS MURDOCH
> *Nuns and Soldiers* (1980)

Mrs. M. is fifty-six years old and has been suffering from insomnia for a long time. When she goes to bed at eleven o'clock, she lies awake for an hour or two, while the events of the day and problems go round and round in her head: frictions with her co-workers, a large dentist's bill that will soon have to be paid, her mother's poor health. She is unable to relax, and instead keeps mulling over all these things, so that sleep refuses to come. Every night when Mrs. M. goes to bed, she is afraid that she will not be able to sleep again. Her alarm clock rings at 6:30 in the morning. She has to get up, even though she feels miserable and exhausted. During the day she cannot keep her mind on her work; she is grouchy, short-tempered, and nervous. She often thinks, "If only I could get a few good nights' rest, I'd be a different person." She has already tried various remedies to cure her insomnia. For a while she took the sleeping pills her doctor prescribed. The pills put her to sleep more quickly, but on the next day she felt tired and unpleasantly "drugged." Once she even fell asleep in the bus on the way to work. After some time the pills began to lose their effectiveness, and she tried to do without them. But once she stopped taking the medication, the nights were worse than ever. She lay awake until three in the morning, and when she finally did fall asleep, she woke up again after only a short while.

Mrs. M. is not alone with her problem. Millions of people lie awake night after night and wait in vain for some refreshing sleep. In a survey taken among the middle-aged population of Switzerland, more than half of the people polled responded that they suffered from insomnia at least occasionally. Seven percent of the men and 12 percent of the women answered that they slept badly almost every night. These figures correspond quite closely to surveys taken in other countries. An American survey of adults indicated that in 6 percent of the subjects the insomnia was so severe that they consulted a doctor. In half of these cases the doctor prescribed sleeping pills.

In all the surveys two findings are particularly striking: (1) sleep disorders are more prevalent among women than among men, and (2) they become more frequent with age. The problems generally take three different forms; sometimes they occur separately, but all three can also occur together. The most common complaint is a difficulty in falling asleep; a person like Mrs. M. may lie awake suffering torments, in extreme cases for hours on end. Whereas good sleepers go to bed and are fast asleep within a few minutes, people with sleep problems wait in vain for sleep to come to them. They toss and turn, hearing the clock strike the hours, and simply cannot fall asleep. A second form of disturbance consists of waking up frequently during the night. People with this trouble sleep too superficially and they wake up repeatedly. Usually they fall asleep again quickly, but sometimes they suffer from lying awake in the middle of the night. A third type of problem is waking up too early in the morning, as when someone wakes up at 4 A.M. and cannot go back to sleep.

When a person's sleep in a sleep laboratory is recorded, by means of the methods described in chapter 2, it is possible to confirm objectively the existence of a sleep disorder either of type 1 (difficulty falling asleep) or types 2 and 3 (difficulty staying asleep). Some people, it turns out, need an abnormally long time to fall asleep, experience interrupted sleep, or have a shortened total sleep period (see figure 6.1). An interesting phenomenon is that the claim "I didn't sleep a wink all night" is

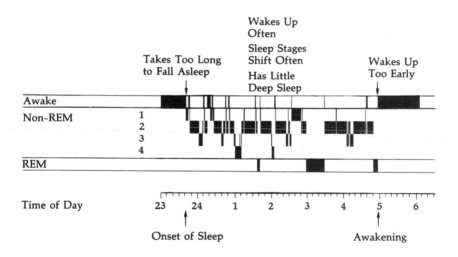

FIGURE 6.1

Sleep Disturbance.

An example of a case in which a patient had difficulty both in falling asleep and in staying asleep. The sleep profile indicates that the patient could not fall asleep for forty minutes after going to bed, woke up several times during the night, and could not fall asleep again after 5 A.M. In addition, the percentage of deep sleep (stages 3 and 4) is small, and the shifts from one sleep stage to another occur with increased frequency.

seldom literally true: the laboratory recordings show that people who make such a statement did in fact sleep for several hours. Often such people overestimate the time it took them to fall asleep. For example, in a large-scale study, patients with sleep disorders said that they needed more than an hour to fall asleep on the average, although the recordings revealed the period to be less than thirty minutes. Can we conclude from such tests that these people with sleep problems are "malingerers" who invent their symptoms?

This would be an erroneous assumption. Poor sleep is a complaint based on subjective experience, just like pain, and it would be pointless to use objective measurements to disprove what such patients feel. If a person complains of insufficient or unrefreshing sleep, then his or her statements should be taken seriously, even when they cannot be measured or objectively verified.

Discrepancies between the subjective and the objective quality of sleep pose an extremely interesting question, albeit one we cannot yet answer very satisfactorily: What factors contribute to a feeling of having slept well, so that one is refreshed in the morning? It would appear that people respond very subjectively to the experience of sleep. Otherwise it would be difficult to understand why some people are quite content with their sleep, although recordings show it to be brief and frequently interrupted, while others complain of having slept badly in spite of an objective lack of abnormalities. A great step forward would be taken if scientists could find a connection between objective, measurable categories (such as certain EEG patterns) and the subjective experience of how good or poor sleep has been, but so far all such attempts have failed.

The possibility exists that people with sleep disorders represent a sector of the population with a particular sensitivity to changes in their sleep; they may also be particularly affected by sleep deprivation and react more negatively to it than others do. According to one hypothesis, the body functions of such people may remain activated even after they have fallen asleep, with the result that their sleep, whose occurrence can be objectively verified, is not experienced as sleep. A final subcategory of people who sleep badly must be mentioned: those who suffer from feelings of depression and anxiety, and whose insomnia must be regarded as a symptom of a more general psychological disturbance.

The causes of disturbed sleep are thus extremely varied. In the Swiss survey referred to above, the most frequently named cause was not being able to get certain thoughts out of one's head. One young woman cannot sleep because of problems with her boyfriend; Mrs. M. is unable to stop worrying about conflicts at work, financial troubles, and her mother's health. Business executives cannot leave the stress of their job behind them and lie awake at night preparing the next morning's meeting in their heads. Although they are exhausted, they are not able to fall asleep. For them, as for Macbeth, the "sleep that knits up the ravell'd sleeve of care, . . . sore labour's bath, Balm of hurt minds," refuses to put in its longed-for appearance.[1] Sometimes sleep is delayed not by worries but by pleasurable anticipation. On the evening before her birthday, my eight-year-old daughter appeared in the living room at midnight and explained that she simply could not fall asleep: "I'm so excited about tomorrow!"

At other times it is illness that disturbs our sleep: pain keeps sick people from sleeping, although they have an urgent need for this "balm." Alternatively, the cause may be a bad cough, or difficulty in breathing, both of which can wake us up repeatedly during the night.

For healthy people sleep is often disturbed by conditions in the environment. City dwellers may experience the roar of traffic just outside their bedroom windows as a constant disturber of their nightly rest. In the Swiss survey mentioned earlier, the noise of cars and airplanes was the most frequently named cause of regularly occurring sleep disturbances. Quiet surroundings at night have obviously become a luxury that many people must do without in today's world.

Finally, the weather must be mentioned as a factor contributing to insomnia, even though it is not easy to pin down its effect. The survey in Switzerland showed *"Föhn* and changes in the weather"* to be the second most frequently mentioned cause of occasional sleep disturbances. One of the few studies of this problem indicated that both very low barometric pressure and very high pressure can tend to make people sleepy in the daytime. Unfortunately, not enough is known about the correlation between weather and sleep. In particular, we do not yet know why some people react so sensitively to changes in the weather, while others do not even notice them.

Most people can confirm from their own experience that they sleep best in familiar surroundings, where they feel secure and at home. A strange bed in a hotel room and unfamiliar noises can contribute to a poor night's rest. Subjects under observation in a sleep laboratory usually do not sleep well on the first night. They take a longer time to fall asleep, the first REM sleep episode is delayed, and they often wake up for brief intervals during the night. For this reason the first night is used to let subjects adapt to the laboratory surroundings and is not considered part of the experiment.

Not only do conditions during the night affect sleep but also how one spends the hours before bedtime. It is not a good idea to indulge in physically or mentally strenuous activities in the evening; and heavy meals can disturb sleep, especially if they are combined with large amounts of alcohol, coffee, and nicotine. The importance of the time at which one goes to bed will be discussed in detail in the chapter on biological rhythms.

Up to now we have dealt with instances in which the causes of insomnia are rather clearly defined. However, people often

*Translator's note: The *Föhn* is a weather phenomenon of northern Switzerland and southern Germany; it occurs when southerly winds push a high-pressure area over the natural barrier of the Alps from Italy. The sudden change in barometric pressure causes many people to complain of headaches, inability to concentrate, and circulation problems. Since the *Föhn* usually brings Italian weather with it—sunshine, bright blue skies, and warmer temperatures—sometimes after days on end of northern European gray and rain, it is hard for people who are not weather sensitive to understand what all the fuss is about.

sleep poorly even though clear causes cannot be identified. This is especially true of the elderly, who are no longer able to remain asleep for hours at a stretch. As people grow old, their sleep obviously becomes more fragmented and frequently interrupted; many elderly people experience such age-related changes in their sleep pattern as a disturbance, but this need not always be so.

When patients complain of severe sleep problems of unknown origin, physicians need to establish whether the cause may not be an underlying psychological problem. Insomnia is often the first sign of depression, which may be covert and as such not immediately recognizable. The treatment of these patients should concentrate on the actual illness and not on the symptom of insomnia alone. The relation between sleep and depression will concern us again in another context in chapters 11 and 12. However, in addition to depression other forms of psychological or mental disorders as well as addictions (such as alcoholism) are often accompanied by insomnia.

Ways to Improve Sleep

What can people do who have trouble sleeping? Should they consult a doctor or try home remedies? Are sleeping pills the only really effective solution, or do other possibilities exist? Can insomnia damage their health? These are some of the questions that sleep researchers hear over and over again. Let us address the last question first. Some people become concerned if they sleep badly for a night or two, and worry that their health will be affected. Such fears are groundless. Almost everyone experiences occasional short episodes of poor sleep; usually, no particular treatment is required, and there is no evidence that transient periods of insomnia have a deleterious effect on a person's general condition or health. If insomnia becomes more severe and occurs more frequently, it is necessary to search for possible causes. Do I have problems that I cannot put out of my mind? Are tensions in my personal or professional life having a negative effect on my sleep? Are demanding or strenuous tasks filling my evening hours, with the result that the problems go round and round in my head at night? Or do I smoke too much in the evening, and is this why I can't sleep?

Sometimes we can significantly improve sleep just by following the rules of "sleep hygiene":

1. *Establish a regular bedtime.* Sleep is part of a biological twenty-four-hour rhythm (see chapter 11) and should therefore occupy the same phase of each cycle. Irregular sleeping hours can have a negative influence on sleep.

2. *Reserve the evening hours for leisure activities and relaxation.* Strenuous physical or mental activities can contribute to poor sleep. Heavy meals in the evening are also best avoided.

3. *Avoid naps.* People who have trouble sleeping at night should not take naps during the day, so as not to reduce their need for sleep at night.

4. *Avoid caffeine, alcohol, and nicotine.* Drinks containing caffeine (coffee, tea, Coca-Cola) and heavy smoking have a stimulating effect on the nervous system and should be avoided in the evening hours. Although a glass of wine or beer can help some people fall asleep, large amounts of alcohol are detrimental.

5. *Create favorable conditions for sleep.* Good rest can be aided by a quiet, dark room that is not overheated and has a good circulation of air. The bed should be large enough to allow stretching and movement. Many people prefer to lie on a flat, firm mattress.

These simple principles alone can improve the quality of sleep. However, if sleep is still interrupted at night, it is advisable to get up and do something else, such as reading or knitting, instead of lying awake in bed. In case of severe and prolonged insomnia, a doctor should definitely be consulted.

Various exercises or techniques for relaxing are recommended as a help in falling asleep. Their use rests on the assumption that many sleep problems arise from a persistent activation of the organism, which takes the form of excessive muscle tension, too fast a pulse, and a slightly elevated temperature. These assumptions are not based on sufficient evidence, however, since a cause-and-effect relationship between activation of the organism and insomnia has not yet been established.

Relaxation techniques aim to reduce overactive body functions. One of the most familiar forms of this kind of therapy is "autogenic training," a technique that teaches people to concentrate on producing sensations of heaviness and warmth in their limbs and that results in a calming relaxation of the muscles. Related techniques include "progressive relaxation" and "EMG biofeedback training." The latter method consists of recording the electrical activity of the voluntary muscles (EMG = electromyogram) and signaling its intensity to the subject with a buzzer (thus the term *feedback*). The subject must learn to keep the buzzer from sounding for ever longer periods of time and so improve his ability to relax. Although some patients have been successfully treated with these methods, they have not proved to be helpful for all types of insomnia. This is also true of psychotherapy, which focuses on conflicts assumed to underlie the sleep disturbance. Accurately assessing the therapeutic effectiveness of those forms of sleep therapy that do not involve medication is a difficult task, since the causes of insomnia are manifold and since objective criteria for measuring improvement are not easy to find. General conclusions about the merits of these techniques cannot yet be drawn. All of them, though, share one definite advantage, namely, that they do not run the risks or have the side effects of drug therapy. Another positive factor is the circumstance that these methods stimulate insomniacs to become active and to deal with their problems themselves, rather than waiting passively for help from outside. Treatment with sleeping pills demands very little initiative on the part of patients; they swallow the prescribed medication and wait for chemistry to do the rest. Taking these pills night after night, they become convinced that they could not sleep without them. This convenient "pharmacological crutch" can lead to permanent dependency, as patients do not try to search for the causes of their insomnia themselves. It should be emphasized again that sleeping pills are not a cure but only a temporary relief measure. Just as in the case of pain, the use of medication should be considered as a first step only, to be followed by the actual treatment of the patient's disease.

Sleepwalking (Somnambulism)

The sleepwalker balancing on the roof or cliff edge with closed eyes and outstretched arms is a classic feature of cartoons. A number of myths surround this strange state, which seems to combine aspects of waking and sleeping in a paradoxical manner. For a long time scientists assumed that sleepwalkers are in the grip of their dreams and are acting out the events in them; however, recent studies have not confirmed this theory. Sleep laboratory recordings revealed that sleepwalking begins in deep sleep (stages 3 and 4), when dreaming is rare. Subjects remain in deep sleep if the sleepwalking episode is brief; in the course of longer episodes, the EEG changes to look more like the pattern of someone who is awake or just falling asleep. The intensity and length of sleepwalking activity can vary considerably. In the mildest form, a person merely sits up in bed, mutters a few—usually incomprehensible—words, and immediately lies down again. If the episode is longer, sleepwalkers get out of bed, walk around the room, and may even get dressed. Their eyes are open in most cases, and they have a rigid expression on their face. It is clear that sleepwalkers can see, since they are able to avoid bumping into furniture or other obstacles. They can give monosyllabic answers to simple questions. Frequently they lie down again somewhere else, such as in the bathtub, and are very surprised to wake up in unfamiliar surroundings in the morning.

It is a popular misconception, however, that sleepwalkers have a heightened awareness of danger. Accidents happen quite often, and the risk of injury is one of the most serious aspects of this state. On occasion sleepwalkers have fallen out of windows, presumably because they mistook them for doors. Some people who know that they tend to walk in their sleep take precautions when they go to bed; they may put a pail of cold water next to the bed, or tie one end of a cord around their waists and the other end around the bedpost. Unfortunately, even such drastic measures do not always work, since a sleepwalker can easily avoid stepping into the pail and is even capable of untying the cord in his sleep. Sleepwalking occurs relatively often among children; one can even cause it intentionally by picking up a child in deep sleep and standing him on his feet. The cause of sleepwalking is still unknown, but since this form of sleep disorder runs in families, there is probably an inherited tendency. Ordinarily sleepwalking ceases of its own accord as children grow to adulthood.

In a certain sense sleepwalking is the opposite of dreaming. When we dream, we experience a rich and colorful world, in which strange events can take place, but—with the exception of brief twitches and rapid eye movements—our muscle tension disappears completely. By contrast, sleepwalkers move about almost like people who are awake, but they are in a dreamless twilight state of which they retain no memory at all the next morning. The existence of the two states of sleepwalking and dreaming demonstrates quite strikingly that sleep is not a uniform condition but comprises a wide range of different states, including experiences and activities similar to those of wakefulness.

Narcolepsy and Hypersomnia

Narcolepsy is a disturbance of the waking state characterized by irresistible sleep attacks during the day. While it is not a common disease, affecting only one person in every one or two thousand, the total number of narcoleptics is nonetheless considerable. (In the United States, for instance, it is thought to be about one hundred thousand.) Narcolepsy, too, tends to run in families, leading scientists to think that an inherited predisposition exists.

Let us look at a case reported by the American sleep researcher Peter Hauri. R. was a thirty-six-year-old farmer who from the age of seventeen on fell asleep three times a day for ten to fifteen minutes. His friends attributed this oddity to his basic laziness, but R.'s condition was accompanied by a further peculiarity: every time his children made him angry, so that he wanted to scold or punish them, he suddenly felt weak in the knees and had to sit down or even fell down on the floor. R. himself viewed this weakness as a psychological problem and sought help from a psychotherapist. R. was examined at a sleep clinic, and his sleep during the day was recorded. It emerged that R. entered REM sleep immediately from waking, which happens very rarely among healthy people. This observation, in connection with the rest of R.'s medical history, confirmed the diagnosis of narcolepsy, which could then be successfully treated with medication.

The most striking symptom of narcolepsy is the irresistible urge to sleep, which can occur several times a day. After the patient has slept for a brief period, he wakes up again feeling refreshed. Not only the waking state, however, but nighttime sleep as well may be seriously affected. Figure 6.2 illustrates the rest/activity pattern of a healthy person and a narcoleptic, as recorded over a one-month period. These recordings were made in collaboration with Dr. Albert Wettstein of the Neurology Clinic at the University Hospital in Zurich, and demonstrate

Days

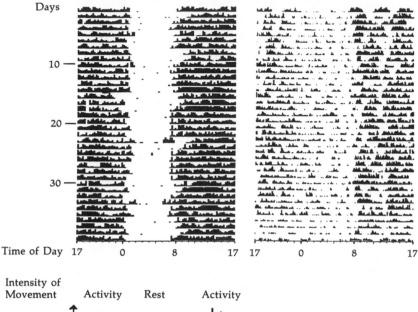

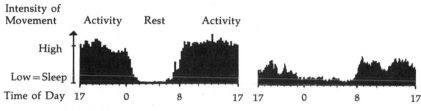

FIGURE 6.2

Rest/Activity Rhythm of a Narcoleptic and a Healthy Person.

Narcoleptics suffer from irresistible urges to sleep during the day and from disturbed sleep at night. The rest/activity rhythm of both the narcoleptic and the healthy person were recorded continuously for one month. Every horizontal line corresponds to one day (from 5 P.M. to 5 P.M. on the following day). The recording begins with the top line. The waking activity of the narcoleptic is repeatedly interrupted by brief periods of sleep. The nights show an unusual amount of activity (motion) as a result of the disturbed sleep. Daytime and nighttime activity of the narcoleptic do not show a large difference; this stands in strong contrast to the clear demarcations between rest and activity in the healthy subject. The same phenomenon appears in the lower diagram, which represents the average curve for the entire recording period. (From a study performed in collaboration with Dr. A. Wettstein.)

strikingly the frequent sleep episodes during the day and the disturbed sleep of the narcoleptic at night. Clearly demarcated rest and activity phases are present in the healthy subject, but not in the narcoleptic patient.

Narcoleptic sleep attacks can occur at the most inconvenient moments, such as at mealtimes or on bicycle rides, or even during sexual intercourse. This can lead to certain problems in interpersonal relations, especially when, as in R.'s case, the abnormality is attributed not to disease but to the personality of the patient. Sleep attacks can, but need not always, be accompanied by other symptoms. As R.'s case history showed, a sudden weakness of the muscles can occur ("cataplexy," in medical terminology). Typically, such weakness is triggered by strong emotions like anger, tears, or laughter. Even a funny joke can cause a narcoleptic to lose muscle tension in his legs and fall to the ground. He remains conscious and can get up again after a few seconds.

Healthy people can also experience the feeling of "going weak in the knees" after a fright or on hearing a piece of very bad news. It thus appears that this normal reaction is pathologically overdeveloped in narcoleptics. Another phenomenon that occurs in mild form among healthy people, but more extremely among narcoleptics, is "sleep paralysis." Patients are unable to move as they are falling asleep or waking up; they feel paralyzed for a period of anywhere from a few seconds to several minutes, a condition accompanied by strong feelings of anxiety. An external touch can cause this symptom to vanish. Narcoleptic patients also often report having particularly vivid dreamlike experiences when they are falling asleep or waking up, which are sometimes associated with feelings of anxiety.

The cause of narcolepsy is unknown. The characteristic features of these sleep attacks and their concomitant symptoms suggest that an imbalance between REM sleep and waking is present. The fact that daytime sleep attacks begin with REM sleep, the sudden loss of muscle tension (cataplexy), the occurrence of sleep paralysis, and vivid dreams all indicate that in narcoleptics the waking state is not sufficiently differentiated from REM sleep. That this disturbance is not limited to human beings was recently demonstrated when narcolepsy was observed in a breed of dogs.

Let us now consider another form of sleep disturbance by examining an individual case. S. suffers from excessive drowsiness in the daytime. Since he was a child, he has had the greatest difficulty waking up and had to be shaken for minutes on end before he could get up. As a boy he built himself an extremely loud alarm clock, since an ordinary one would not wake him up. The racket of this special alarm woke up all the rest of his family, and even the neighbors, but S. slept on. If he finally succeeded in getting up, he staggered around "punch-drunk" from sleepiness and had trouble staying awake. He remained sleepy all day. Although he took long naps, he still did not feel well rested in the afternoon. This medical history suggests that S. is suffering from an excessive need to sleep (hypersomnia). The causes of this disturbance have not been discovered either, but once again it appears that the organism's sleep/wake system is out of balance.

Snoring and Sleep Apnea

PATIENT: "Doctor, what should I do? I snore so loudly that I wake myself up at night."

DOCTOR: "Take these pills before you go to bed, and if they don't help, try sleeping in another room."

Snoring is a favorite subject of jokes and funny stories, but sharing a bed with a spouse who snores too loudly can be grounds for marital discord or even divorce. One man reportedly sued his wife for causing him bodily injury. She testified in her own defense that she had listened to the unbearably loud snoring of her husband for as long as she could stand it. Then she asked him three times to roll over on his stomach. When he failed to comply, she tapped him lightly on the head with a billy club. According to a survey by the World Health Organization in Italy, 10 percent of all adults snore so loudly that they can be heard in the next room. This is referred to as "heroic" or "epic" snoring. Measurements have recorded volumes of up to eighty decibels, a noise level corresponding to that of a jackhammer or pneumatic drill. Polls have shown that about 31 percent of all men and 19 percent of all women snore every night. Intense snoring occurs primarily in deep sleep and decreases or stops altogether in REM sleep. It also increases with age.

How does this annoying sound arise? As we have already seen, muscle tension drops after we have fallen asleep. Especially if we are lying on our back, our tongue and lower jaw slide slightly backward, and this can impede the air flow from the nasal cavity. The result is that we breathe through our mouth. The quick intake of air causes the tissue of the upper airway (the soft palate) to vibrate, and these vibrations become audible as snoring. Overweight people have an especially strong tendency to snore. Their obesity forces them to sleep on their backs, and the excess of fatty tissue in their throats increases the vibrations. One effective treatment for snoring is to lose weight. Sometimes the use of a "snore ball" is recommended; this treatment involves sewing a small, hard spherical object, such as a golf ball, into the back of the snorer's pajama top, and so preventing him from sleeping on his back. Chin straps are also used as antisnore devices. Recently a "snore-feedback" machine was invented; it reacts to the sound of snoring by giving the sleeper a mild electric shock.

Diseases can also cause changes in the airways that lead to snoring: colds, allergies, and sinus problems can all impede breathing; in children enlarged tonsils may have the same effect. It was not until recently that another, quite serious condition was discovered: in some instances snoring is a symptom of a disorder known as sleep apnea (a-pnea, from the Greek term for "without breath").

Sleep apnea is a breathing disturbance that takes the form of recurrent periods of respiratory arrest during sleep. These may occur several hundred times a night; they usually last for only a few seconds but may in extreme cases last as long as two minutes. When the patient stops breathing, he becomes increasingly restless and twists about convulsively in bed, but he does not wake up. As breathing resumes, it is accompanied by a loud, explosive snoring sound. Apnea patients are typically obese males over the age of forty; the disorder is rarer among women. During the episodes of respiratory arrest the upper airway becomes blocked and makes it impossible for the patients to inhale. This obstruction (occlusion) most probably occurs as a result of an abnormal drop in the muscle tension of the throat (pharyngeal cavity). Although the cause of this problem has not yet been specified, hereditary tendencies are once again thought to play a role.

Sleep apnea may have two different consequences. Most apnea patients feel drowsy during the day, to such an extreme and disturbing degree that they usually consult a doctor. Daytime drowsiness is probably the result of the frequent respiratory disturbances that lead to a sleep deficit. But apnea has yet another and more serious consequence: during the periods of respiratory arrest the blood level of oxygen drops, which may produce a prolonged oxygen deficiency in the body. This may lead to an increased blood pressure in the pulmonary circulation and to irregularities of the heart rhythm. Both sleeping pills and alcohol aggravate sleep apnea, since they depress respiration during sleep even more. Sleep apnea may be a factor in cases of sudden death that occur in older, overweight people during sleep. Unfortunately it is difficult to treat this problem. Weight loss can have a beneficial effect. In the most serious cases a tracheotomy (an incision in the windpipe) must be performed, in order to ensure that the patient can breathe at night.

Respiratory arrest during sleep may also occur in children and is thought to be the cause of sudden "crib death" in infants (sudden infant death syndrome, or SIDS). Hereditary factors seem to be involved, since according to statistics the siblings of a SIDS victim are the children who are most at risk. Some studies indicate that such children wake up less easily from non-REM sleep and for this reason may be more likely to become victims of respiratory arrest. Various research teams are hard at work investigating the problem, and it is to be hoped that the causes of these tragic deaths will soon be found, and effective ways developed to prevent them.

Of the almost seventy different types of sleeping and waking disorders, only a few have been discussed here. Disorders resulting from disturbances of biological rhythms (for example, those related to shift work) will be covered in chapter 11. But the examples mentioned here should suffice to make us aware that the functions of sleeping and waking cannot be taken for granted; we cannot always count on peaceful, undisturbed, and restorative nighttime sleep or on being refreshed and rested in the morning. Sleep disorders are rarely life-threatening, but since they can affect the quality of our lives in subtle and persistent ways, they must be taken seriously.

7

Sleep in Animals

... that all animals partake in sleep is obvious from the
following considerations. The animal is defined by the
possession of sensation, and we hold that sleep is in some
way the immobilization or fettering of sensation, and that
the release or relaxation of this is waking.

—ARISTOTLE
"On Sleeping and Waking"
Parva Naturalia

We often speak of having "slept like a log," but in some languages comparisons with the sleep of hibernating animals are
common.* The metaphor is appealing: an animal curled up in
its burrow or nest, covered by its thick fur, evokes images of
warmth and security that we associate with good sleep. Are
such agreeable visions based on fact? Do hamsters or groundhogs really spend the winter in a state comparable to the deep
sleep of human beings? As we shall see in the last section of this
chapter, hibernation is not the same as our nightly sleep, nor
does the dormant winter state of the brown bear, which is not
hibernation in the strict sense, really compare to the sleep of
human beings. The use of parallels between human sleep and
the world of animals is only a manner of speaking; we should
not humanize animal sleep by projecting our own sensations
into sleeping creatures. Systematic observations and recording

*Translator's note: In Germany people say after a good night's sleep that
they slept like a marmot (groundhog) or a bear.

of sleep stages provide more objective information about which animals sleep when and how.

Foxes, Rats, and Elephants—Sleep in Mammals

Before going to sleep, a fox digs up the ground and begins to circle around on this spot, first in one direction and then in the other; its muzzle almost touches the tip of its tail. With this behavior the fox creates a small hollow in which to lie. Then it sits down, curls up its tail toward its head, and at last lies down. The upper part of the body and head are curved toward the base of the tail. Finally the fox lifts its head briefly and drops it again, and pushes its muzzle under its tail.

This kind of "sleep ritual," which has been described by the zoologist Liselore Hassenberg, occurs in many other animals as well. Clearly, animals do not abruptly lie down to sleep in just any place; it appears instead that they prepare themselves for sleep with a series of preliminary actions. Every animal has its own, characteristic place for sleeping. Foxes and bears prefer protected spots, such as caves; the monk seal has found a most original solution to the problem: it sleeps in caves in oceanfront cliffs, which are situated high enough to be dry but which can be entered only from under water. There it can sleep in safety, undisturbed. Rodents withdraw to their nests to sleep—nests that hamsters dig in the ground and squirrels build in trees. Some anthropoid apes also sleep in trees, but they seek out a different place each night. It is known that certain birds (such as the guinea fowl) withdraw to their "sleep trees" in the evening, in order to spend the night as part of a group.

Animals, like people, have preferred positions for sleeping, some of which are illustrated in figure 7.1. Cats sleep on their side, either stretched out or rolled up. Kangaroos also sleep on their side, while other animals curl up on their belly (rabbits, foxes, horses). The hyena shown in the illustration sleeps face

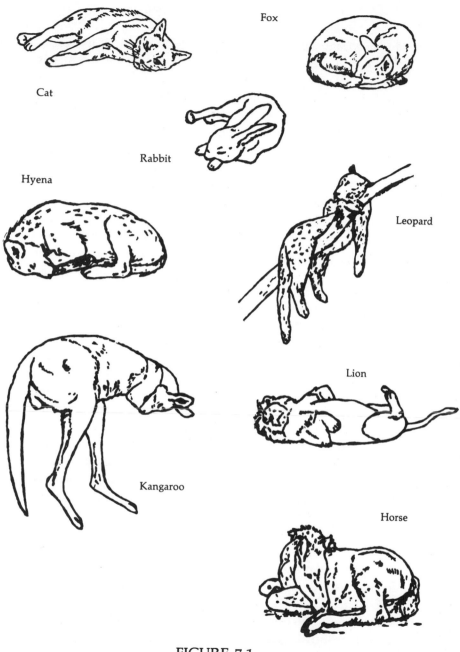

FIGURE 7.1

Sleep Positions of Animals.

SOURCE: From L. Hassenberg, *Ruhe und Schlaf bei Säugetieren* (Ziemsen Verlag: Wittenberg Lutherstadt, 1965). With the kind permission of L. Hassenberg.

down, with its entire body curled up from the tip of its nose to the tail; this position lets the animal roll itself up completely into a ball. Lions are among the few animals who prefer to sleep on their backs; rabbits and bears sometimes do this as well. The leopard is shown asleep in a straddling position on the branch of a tree, with its legs and tail dangling. The position favored by bats, hanging head down, is even more striking. Observations thus show that different types of animals have their own, characteristic sleep positions. But do other mammals display the same stages of sleep typical of human beings?

To answer this question we must make use of recordings of electric brain waves (EEG). Like that of human beings, the EEG of an animal can be registered by means of metal electrodes attached to the skull or positioned on the surface of the brain. Figure 7.2 illustrates the electric potentials of a rat's brain and muscles during waking and sleeping, and the different sleep stages. The patterns recorded for the rat clearly resemble those of man. When the rat is awake, the waves are small and exhibit a regular rhythm of approximately seven cycles per second (theta rhythm). The relatively high tension of the voluntary muscles produces large, rapid waves in the muscle recording (EMG). After the rat has fallen asleep, the muscles relax. During non-REM sleep the EEG shows large, slow, and irregular waves, while during REM sleep the waves become smaller, more rapid, and more regular. REM sleep is characterized not only by rapid eye movements but also by sporadic twitching of the rat's whiskers and paws. Stages of REM and non-REM sleep can be observed in practically all mammals that have been studied so far. The only exceptions are dolphins and spiny anteaters (echidnas, which belong to the lowest order of mammals, the monotremes). No REM sleep has been observed in them. Different stages of sleep, accompanied by the typical changes in EEG patterns, are therefore characteristic of most mammals.

Let us return to the rat and take a closer look at its sleep. The rat is a nocturnal animal and gets most of its sleep in the daytime. Sleep recordings over twenty-four hours showed that rats

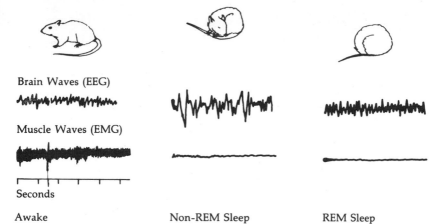

Brain Waves (EEG)

Muscle Waves (EMG)

Seconds

Awake   Non-REM Sleep   REM Sleep

FIGURE 7.2.
Sleep Stages in Mammals.

Waking and the sleep stages can be discriminated in all mammals from recordings of electrical brain and muscle activity. The EEG of a rat shows small, rapid waves during waking and during REM sleep; the EEG shows large, slow waves during non-REM sleep. The muscle tension (EMG) measured in the rat's neck drops sharply during sleep. In addition, rapid eye movements occur during REM sleep.

sleep about twelve hours, ten of them in non-REM sleep and two in REM sleep. However, rats do not spend the entire day (which corresponds to the night in terms of human sleep) sleeping, but are awake for more than two hours. Like many other animals, the rat displays "polyphasic" sleep, which is frequently interrupted by periods of wakefulness. A single sleep episode typically lasts for only a few minutes, and the following waking episode also tends to be brief. In animals, just as in man, sleep begins with non-REM sleep and then progresses into REM sleep. Since a single non-REM/REM sleep cycle lasts only ten minutes in rats, their individual sleep stages are much shorter than those of human beings.

The proportions of sleep and wakefulness vary among mammals, and we can find both short and long sleepers. The bat, which spends twenty out of every twenty-four hours asleep, certainly belongs in the latter category, as do the oppossum (eighteen to nineteen hours) and the porcupine (seventeen to eighteen hours). By contrast cows, horses, and elephants make do with only three to four hours of sleep a day. (Longer periods of sleep have been reported for elephants in some cases.) No direct connection appears to exist between the total sleep time and the amount of REM sleep. A horse, which sleeps only three hours a day, spends 20 percent of this time in REM sleep; a mole with eight to nine hours of daily sleep spends 25 percent of it in REM sleep, but a mouse (thirteen hours) only 10 percent. Nonetheless, certain general principles can be established. It is equally true of animals and human beings that the percentage of their REM sleep is very high just after birth but declines rapidly during development. Newborn rats, for example, spend 72 percent of their sleep in REM sleep but mature rats only 15–20 percent. We observe similar proportions in cats. In guinea pigs, which are born at a much more mature state, the percentage of REM sleep is far lower at birth than in rats or cats and declines correspondingly less in the following weeks. It thus appears that the high percentage of REM sleep in the early stages of life is related to the stage of development. It should be noted that it is more difficult to discriminate the sleep stages in newborn animals than in mature ones.

A number of experiments have been conducted to compare the sleep habits of different animals and to see whether connections can be established with other physiological or behavioral characteristics. Such comparative studies have produced interesting results on the relationship between sleep and metabolism. Small animals, which generally have a high metabolic rate and a short life span, sleep longer than larger animals with a lower metabolism and longer life expectancy. (Porcupines live to be about six years old, for instance, whereas horses live about forty-six years.) The length of the non-REM/REM sleep cycle is also related, so that small animals with low brain weight and high metabolism have a shorter cycle than larger animals. The average duration of the non-REM/REM sleep cycle is 10 minutes in rats, 28 minutes in cats, 90 minutes in human beings, and 120 minutes in elephants. Simplifying somewhat, we can say that a short, intensive life goes hand in hand with a long total sleep period and a short sleep cycle. As always, there are many exceptions to this "rule."

Putting these somewhat theoretical questions aside and returning to concrete examples, we can approach the subject of animals' sleep from yet another angle. Hoofed animals like cows, horses, sheep, and pigs spend a great deal of time dozing, a condition that is not considered to belong to the category of sleep as such. A cow sleeps only four hours a day, but spends another eight dozing—lying down, but with its head and neck erect. The EEG of a cow in this condition contains both the rapid waves characteristic of waking and the slower waves typical of non-REM sleep. Cows go on chewing their cud while dozing, and this activity can even continue on into actual sleep. Obviously the borderline between waking and sleeping is not clear-cut in many animals. Cows also demonstrate the strong influence of environmental factors on the sleep stages. The French researcher Yves Ruckebusch has reported that a cow kept in a barn spends 40 minutes per day in REM sleep, a cow living in a meadow only 20 minutes. If the cow is brought back to the barn after spending five weeks in the fields, its REM sleep increases temporarily, up to 110 minutes a day, and then gradually drops again to the normal quota of 40 minutes. The time spent outdoors appears to have induced a REM sleep deficit, which is compensated for in the succeeding days.

In conclusion we will take a look at one of the few mammals that have developed the highly specialized ability to live in water. Dolphins that can attain a weight of four hundred pounds live in the Black Sea. EEG recordings of these animals revealed a surprising phenomenon: during a sleep episode, which usually lasts from thirty to sixty minutes, only one-half of the brain showed a typical sleep EEG; the other half produced a waking EEG. Then the two halves reversed their roles: the half that had been "awake" showed a sleep EEG, and the other half "woke up." Simultaneous sleep in both hemispheres of the dolphin's brain was almost never observed. The meaning of this strange division of labor is not yet understood. The studies showed conclusively, though, that the electrical sleep patterns of this animal do not necessarily encompass the entire brain but may occur only in a specific part.

The Origins of Sleep

Figure 7.4 contains a kind of "family tree" illustrating the evolution of life on earth. Scientists assume today that eons ago one-celled creatures came into existence, which then evolved into many-celled forms of life. Did a corresponding evolution of sleep take place? The best way to tackle this problem is not to start at the very top of the tree but to look first at a class of animals that branched off before the mammals did.

Among birds, we find not only definite patterns of sleep

Right Half
of the Brain

Left Half
of the Brain

FIGURE 7.3
The Sleep of a Dolphin.
The right and left halves of a dolphin's brain sleep in alternation.

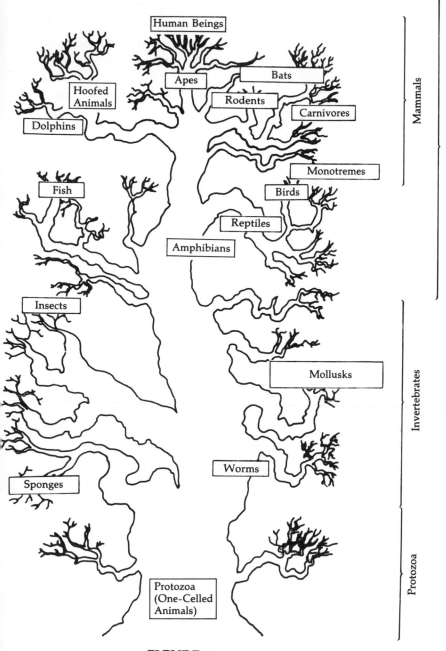

FIGURE 7.4
The Evolution of Life as a Family Tree.

behavior but also the kinds of EEG changes typical of mammals. Pigeons sleep on the average just under ten hours per day; about forty minutes are spent in REM sleep, but the individual REM sleep episodes last only a few seconds. In REM sleep pigeons display both the characteristic EEG pattern and rapid eye movements. The pronounced relaxation of the muscles that accompanies REM sleep in mammals is clearly lacking in most birds, however. An almost total loss of neck muscle tension has been observed only in geese. The English zoologist Dennis Lendrem has reported observations that pigeons open their eyes repeatedly in sleep, presumably in order to be able to recognize the approach of a predator. When pigeons sleep in groups, they open their eyes less frequently, a finding that could be explained by the hypothesis that the group as a whole shares the task of keeping a lookout for danger. One bird can warn all the others, and each bird in a group need not be as alert as when it sleeps by itself. This phenomenon is referred to as corporate vigilance.

Migratory birds present a puzzle of their own. During their migrations they are forced to fly over the open ocean for several days at a time and cannot interrupt their flight to rest. The question is still open whether they do without sleep entirely or are able to sleep while flying or gliding. The answer might provide important information about whether sleep is absolutely essential for higher forms of life.

The class of reptiles can be considered evolutionary forerunners of birds. The American sleep researcher Edward Tauber has given the following description of sleep behavior in chameleons:

> . . . the animal typically settles on a branch in the hours immediately prior to sunset, curls up his tail in watch spring fashion, and remains still; however, constant independent scanning eye movements of widely ranging angular travel persist. During this state prior to sleep, the lizard not only does not attack insects but ignores crickets which alight on

his body. The head and belly come to rest on the branch and the clawed feet assume a loose straddling position in contrast to the tight grasping posture during wakefulness. The eyelids close in a circular manner and the eyeballs are slightly retracted. Unless disturbed, the animal will generally remain in this position throughout the night.[1]

We can see from this example that reptiles can exhibit a definite form of sleep behavior. However, in the few studies in which brain waves were recorded, the pattern differed from that in mammals and birds. It is not readily possible to discriminate the standard sleep stages in reptiles. The same holds for the class of amphibians, to which frogs and toads belong. Since amphibians remain motionless for long periods of time even when awake, direct observation of their behavior is of little help in determining whether they are asleep or not. It is also difficult to distinguish sleep from the torpor that affects cold-blooded animals (such as reptiles and amphibians) at low temperatures.

It is a good deal easier to observe sleep in fish. Like mammals, some species of fish seek out a special place to sleep and assume a characteristic rest position. In this state they no longer react to mild external stimuli, but only to stronger ones. The parrot fish exhibits an interesting peculiarity: before going to sleep, it secretes a protective cover of mucus in which it can hide.

We can sum up what has been said so far by stating that sleep is observable in all vertebrates. To study the case of the more ancient invertebrate animals, let us look again at a particular example. The aplysia, a giant marine snail belonging to the mollusks, was studied by the American scientist Felix Strumwasser. When kept in an aquarium, this animal swims around the tank during the day and spends much of its time searching for food. At sunset it withdraws to a corner and remains still, so that at night only sporadic motions of the head and antennae are visible. In the morning, after sunrise, the slug "wakes up" and commences another period of activity.

Another example of an invertebrate is the moth, which is not constantly in flight but also periodically exhibits brief phases of rest. As these phases progress, stronger and stronger stimuli are required to arouse the animal. There also appears to be a relation between the position assumed by the moth and the "depth" of its "sleep." In the "deepest" state, the antennae are folded on its back and covered by the wings, and even lifting the wings with a small brush will not cause the moth to react. These two examples indicate that phases of inactivity resembling sleep occur in invertebrates as well.

If we consider the alternation of rest and activity phases, on the basis of long-term recordings, we see a twenty-four-hour rhythmicity in most animals. As figure 7.5 shows, the rhythm of rest (white spaces) and activity (dark bars) in human beings, rats, and flies is quite similar, even though the active phase occurs at different times of day. Figure 7.6 gives an example from the plant kingdom: bean plants also exhibit a definite twenty-four-hour periodicity with regard to the position of their leaves. In daylight hours the leaves are extended; during the hours of darkness they droop. As we shall see later, such daily rhythms do not depend solely on cyclical changes in the environment, such as light and darkness, which scientists refer to as *zeitgebers*,* but are caused by a kind of "internal clock" in the organism. This aspect of plant behavior will not concern us further here; it should merely serve to suggest that a connection may exist between daily rhythms and sleep. Processes with a daily periodicity can be observed throughout the animal kingdom, including the simplest one-celled forms of life. It is legitimate to speculate that this twenty-four-hour rest/activity rhythm could be an evolutionary precursor of the sleep/wake cycle. The daily rest periods occurring at certain phases of the rhythm in simple animals might correspond to the sleep period of higher vertebrates. We will deal with sleep as part of a biological rhythm in later chapters, and see that the

*Translator's note: The German term *Zeitgeber* (literally, "time giver") has been taken over in the English terminology of rhythm research, and refers to an external synchronizing factor.

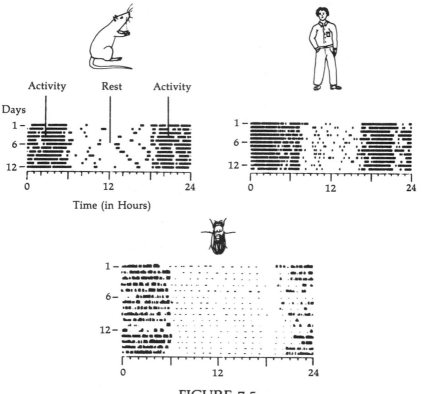

FIGURE 7.5
Rest/Activity Rhythm of Rat, Person, and Fly.

The rest/activity rhythms are similar. Periods of activity are shown as horizontal bars, periods of rest as white spaces. Rats are active at night, people and flies during the day.

The recording of the fly's activity has been adapted from an illustration by J. Aschoff and U. Saint Paul, "Longevity among bowflies phormia terraechovae R. D. kept in non-24-hour light-dark cycles," *Journal of Comparative Physiology* 127 (1978):191–95.

FIGURE 7.6
Twenty-four-Hour Rhythm of Plants (Bean Plant).

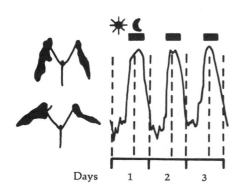

The diagram illustrates the movements of the leaves of a bean plant over a period of three days. The peaks of the curve indicate drooping leaves; the troughs indicate that the leaves are extended. The black bars at the top of the diagram indicate the periods of darkness.

SOURCE: Adapted from E. Bünning, *The Physiological Clock* (Heidelberg: Springer-Verlag, 1973), pp 8–9, figures 4–5.

rhythmic aspect of sleep is a particularly important part of its regulation.

Sleep as a Regulated Process

It has been demonstrated that it becomes increasingly more difficult to distinguish the traditional sleep stages as we move down the evolutionary family tree toward simpler organisms. This is partly because the brain structure of "lower" animals shows little resemblance to that of mammals, so that electric signals recorded in the brains of these different organisms are not comparable. We can observe sleeplike behavior even in simple animals, but we cannot say with certainty whether this behavior should be understood as genuine sleep. In order to shed more light on this question, we must not merely describe sleep but also consider its dynamic or functional aspects. The study of sleep deprivation has proved to be a highly useful technique.

If we consider sleep in the rat from this vantage point, we can observe that it is characterized by a sequence of non-REM and REM sleep stages (see figure 7.7, "Before Sleep Deprivation"). We can use spectral analysis to determine the proportion of slow waves (deep sleep) occurring in non-REM sleep. The peaks in the delta record reflect the deep sleep of the rat, which corresponds to stages 3 and 4 in man. The troughs correspond to periods of REM sleep and wakefulness, in which slow waves are absent. REM sleep episodes are marked by dark bars under the delta plots. Keeping a rat from sleep for twenty-four hours results in an increase in both delta sleep and REM sleep. The higher peaks in the delta record reflect the presence of especially large, slow waves in the EEG. REM sleep episodes are both more frequent and longer after sleep deprivation. Prolonging a rat's wake time thus leads to an intensification of non-REM sleep and an increase in REM sleep.

Before Sleep Deprivation

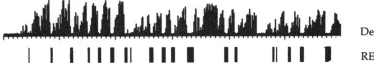

Delta Sleep

REM Sleep

After Sleep Deprivation

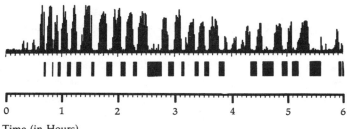

Time (in Hours)

FIGURE 7.7
Sleep Deprivation in a Rat.

Sleep deprivation in rats promotes non-REM sleep with slow EEG waves (delta sleep) and increases the frequency and length of REM sleep episodes. The illustration shows the spectral curves of EEG slow waves (1–4 Hz = delta waves) before and after twenty-four-hour sleep deprivation. REM sleep episodes are shown as dark bars under the curves; they occur in the "valleys" of the spectral curves.

Animals other than rats also react to sleep deprivation in this fashion. We shall see later that the situation is basically similar in man. Sleep thus depends on the duration of prior waking. Apparently, sleep that has been "lost" must be made up for at the next opportunity. Since the length and intensity of sleep are controlled by regulatory mechanisms, this aspect could be useful in investigating sleeplike states in simple organisms.

My colleague Irene Tobler has addressed this problem. She chose to work on cockroaches, since their pronounced rest/activity rhythm makes them good subjects for experiments. The goal was to see whether the existence of a sleeplike process can be established for this animal. In the first tests the normal rest/activity pattern was recorded over a period of several days. Cockroaches are nocturnal creatures that become active in the hours of darkness. The actual experiment then consisted of disturbing the animal with external stimuli for three hours during a rest phase. The consequences of this "rest deprivation" were a reduction of activity in the hours of the night immediately following the disturbance, a reaction corresponding to a mammal's making up for lost sleep after sleep deprivation. To make sure that the results of the experiment were not caused solely by the animal's exhaustion, further experiments were performed in which the cockroach was disturbed only slightly. Longer rest phases were observed even after such minimal interference.

The experiment described above is a first attempt to clarify the evolutionary origins of sleep from the standpoint of sleep regulation. The results suggest that sleep or a condition resembling sleep appeared much earlier in evolution than had previously been supposed.

Hibernation

The winter season poses a threat to many animals. Migratory birds must travel enormous distances in the fall to find warmer regions, but mammals cannot leave their cold climate. Some of them adapt to this challenge by metabolic changes. They enter a sleeplike state, reducing their respiratory rate and circulation to a minimum. Their body temperature may fall close to the freezing point and their metabolism may be reduced to only 10 to 15 percent of its normal rate. This genuine form of hibernation occurs in porcupines, bats, weasels, groundhogs, hamsters, and dormice. In this dormant winter state, such animals live on reserves of stored fat, which are gradually used up. In other

animals—including squirrels, prairie dogs, and brown bears—
what sets in is not true hibernation but a form of torpor during
which temperature, respiration, and heartbeat drop to levels no
lower than those of normal sleep. Most animals withdraw to
their nests or burrows, where they live on their fat reserves as
well as on stored food like nuts.

The first detailed studies of the relationship between sleep
and hibernation were made only recently. Results showed that
animals enter hibernation from non-REM sleep. If a dormouse,
for example, is in a superficial stage of hibernation and its
temperature has not yet dropped sharply, continuous non-REM
sleep can be recorded; REM sleep does not occur at all. More
profound hibernation produces flat brain waves that bear no
resemblance to those of ordinary sleep. The daytime sleep
("lethargy") of the bat is a particularly interesting phenomenon, which is also characterized by a marked drop in body
temperature. Unfortunately, no detailed EEG investigations of
this state have yet been made.

According to our present understanding of daytime or nighttime sleep on the one hand and hibernation on the other, the
two states are fundamentally different phenomena. Nevertheless, non-REM sleep may still exhibit a certain resemblance to
hibernation, since the deep sleep (stages 3 and 4 of human
non-REM sleep) that occurs soon after the onset of sleep is also
characterized by a noticeable drop in temperature as well as by
a slowing of breathing and heart rate. Thus the condition of
quiescence and reduced consciousness in which we spend the
dark and cold hours of the night has some features in common
with the form of "sleep" that permits animals to survive the
dark, cold season of the year. Nevertheless we must conclude
that the fundamental mechanisms underlying hibernation remain to be clarified.

8

Sleep and the Brain

Which came first—the hen or the egg? In the alternation
of sleep and wakefulness, which of the two states inter-
rupts the other? Is the onset of sleep an active process or
a mere cessation of wakefulness?
—NATHANIEL KLEITMAN
Sleep and Wakefulness (1963)

Is Sleep an Active or a Passive Process?

After the First World War a dreaded disease spread through
Europe, the virus infection *Encephalitis lethargica,* which often
resulted in death. Fever and agitation characterized the early
stage of this disease; after a few weeks lethargy and drowsiness
followed, and, above all, unnaturally prolonged sleep. The
question arose about what structure of the brain could be responsible for this pathological need to sleep. When the brain
tissues of patients who had died of the disease were examined
under a microscope, it became evident that the infection was
connected with changes in the cells of the interbrain (dienceph-
alon). Was this the cause of excessive sleep? Later, in the 1920s,
animal experiments enabled scientists to investigate in more
detail the brain structures involved in the regulation of sleep.

At that time the discussion was dominated by one fundamental question, which led to heated controversy among the
experts: Is sleep a passive process arising solely from the cessation of the waking state, as the Roman poet Lucretius already

claimed? Or is it rather an active process, originating in certain brain centers? The Belgian neurophysiologist Frédéric Bremer was a prominent advocate of the first theory. With his experiments during the 1930s he attempted to demonstrate that the state of wakefulness can be maintained only as long as sensory stimuli from the environment impinge upon the brain. After transecting the neural pathways that connect the sensory organs with the brain, Bremer observed a continuous state of sleep in his laboratory animals. This finding lent support to the assumption that sleep is a passive process occurring whenever activating influences are absent.

The most important representative of the opposite theory was Walter Hess, professor of physiology at the University of Zurich and later a Nobel Prize winner in medicine. He was one of the first to develop a technique that made it possible to study the effects of electrical stimuli on behavior by permanently implanting tiny microelectrodes in certain regions of the brains of laboratory animals. Physicians have recently adopted this procedure for treating patients and, in particular, for determining and eliminating an epileptic focus in the brain. Since the brain is not sensitive to pain, neither the implantation nor the electrical stimulation causes the patient any pain.

Hess observed that stimulation of certain regions of the brain would cause the animal to seek out its resting place, assume its typical sleeping position, and fall asleep. Although the animal could be awakened at any time, the arousing stimuli had to reach a certain level of intensity in order to arouse the animal —just as it must with natural sleep. After the electrical stimulation via the electrode, the animal would often remain asleep for hours. When electrodes had been placed at particular places in the interbrain, sleep could be induced especially well.

The findings of Professor Hess cast doubt upon the theory of passive sleep, since in his experiments sleep was induced by the stimulation of the brain, and not just by the removal of an external sensory stimulus. It was characteristic of Hess's integrated view of brain functions that he did not regard sleep as an

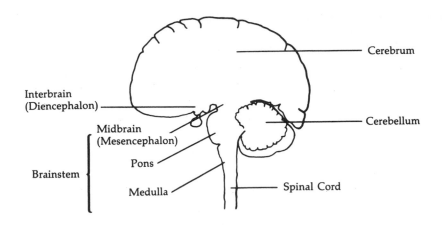

FIGURE 8.1
The Most Important Regions of the Brain.
A longitudinal cross-section of the human brain

isolated process that could be investigated apart from other physiological processes. In 1931 he wrote, "Our own attempt to elucidate the question of the nature of sleep, and its mechanism, is based on the assumption that this problem can *not* be solved *on its own,* but only in terms of an analysis of the *entire functional structure of the organism.* "[1] He distinguished two basic functional states: the ergotropic state (from the Greek words meaning "tending toward work"), which predominates during the day and makes an organism capable of active forms of behavior like attack or flight; and the trophotropic state (a tending toward a "nourishing" or "replenishing," in Greek), which allows the body to conserve energy, to recuperate, and to avoid excessive stress. Hess regarded sleep as "a differentiated function occurring as part of the general trophotropic (parasympathetic) function."[2]

The controversy over the active or passive nature of sleep was revived in the late 1940s, when Giuseppe Moruzzi, a professor at the University of Pisa, and the American physiologist Horace Magoun discovered that electrical stimulation of the brainstem will awaken an animal instantaneously. In order to discuss their experiments, it will be necessary to go into some anatomical detail. There exists an extensive network of nerve cells running longitudinally in the brainstem; its fibers extend into the forebrain as well as down into the spinal cord. It is known as the reticular formation, from the Latin word for "net" *(reticulum)*. Moruzzi's experimental results appeared to suggest that this was the primary activating structure and that stimulating it led to an alert and wakeful condition. Further studies soon showed that the situation was more complicated than that. It could be demonstrated that electrical stimulation of the posterior (caudal) section of the reticular formation did not cause a laboratory animal to wake up but, on the contrary, put it to sleep. The existence of two distinct regions in the brainstem, one promoting sleep and the other inhibiting it, was demonstrated in an elegant experiment. A group of Italian neurophysiologists implanted cannulae (tiny tubes) in the blood vessels supplying the anterior and posterior parts of the brainstem. When they injected an anesthetic into the front vessels, "sleep" resulted, since the activating regions of the brainstem were suppressed. But interestingly enough, when exactly the same substance was injected into the rear vessels, a sleeping animal woke up, because the sleep-promoting structures were inhibited. The identical anesthetic could thus induce sleep or wakefulness, depending on the area it affected!

On the basis of our present-day knowledge, sleep and wakefulness must be considered two different but "equal" states, neither of which can be explained simply as the cessation or lack of the other. Although the activation of certain structures in the brain promotes one or the other state, there is no single "center" of sleeping or waking. If we examine the activity of individual nerve cells in the brain, we find that most of them are active during both sleeping and waking. What changes is their pattern of "firing." Overstating the case only slightly, we could say that our brain does not sleep when we do.

Jouvet's Theory of Monoamines

The brain as a subject for research remained well into the 1960s almost the exclusive domain of physiologists and anatomists. They studied the links between different groups of nerve cells, constructed anatomical "maps," and tried to draw inferences from them about possible brain functions. In physiological studies of the relation between structure and function, one of the most important techniques was the electrical stimulation of specific areas of the brain and the lesion of circumscribed regions. Soon, however, a new procedure became available. It was now possible to implant electrodes permanently in the brain and to record in unanesthetized animals not only global electrical activity but even the firing of individual nerve cells. It was already well known then that electrical impulses do not proceed directly from one nerve cell to the next but are interrupted at junctions called synapses.

There a chemical substance (a neurotransmitter) is released; it crosses the tiny synaptic cleft between two nerve cells and initiates an electrical change in the membrane of the target cell. This process may lead to the generation of a new nerve impulse. The initial investigations of the role of transmitters focused on the peripheral nerves outside the brain, since they were easily accessible, whereas the complex structures of the brain did not lend themselves to the same kind of experiments. However, there were indications even then, in the early sixties, that transmitters are also involved in the transfer of information between nerve cells in the brain.

A breakthrough occurred in 1964, when Swedish scientists succeeded in developing a method for making neurotransmitters visible when one examines in the microscope sections of brain tissue. The "maps" of the brain thereby acquired an additional chemical dimension. The nerve cells that use noradrenaline as a transmitter, for example, could be located in certain nuclei in the brainstem and their extensions (axons) traced into different structures of the forebrain. These new techniques also allowed pharmacologists and biochemists to become serious competitors of anatomists and physiologists in exploring the functions of the brain. Thus a fruitful collaboration between diverse disciplines developed. Pharmacologists were familiar with substances that could be used to inhibit or enhance the effects of certain neurotransmitters. In addition, because many psychoactive drugs are known to influence synaptic transmitters, the mechanisms underlying their therapeutic effects could be investigated. Finally, new methods were developed that made it possible to inject minute amounts of chemical substances into a specific group of nerve cells, in order to effect a chemical stimulation of a small, well-defined brain area. Throughout the world brain research began to advance at a breathtaking rate. Within a short time scientists identified several important transmitters and their pathways in the brain. Those transmitters possessing one amino group are known as monoamines; the most important among them are noradrenaline, dopamine, and serotonin.

Michel Jouvet, a professor of experimental medicine at the University of Lyon (France) and a member of the prestigious French Academy of Science, was one of the first to recognize the importance of these discoveries for sleep research. After he had performed pioneering studies on REM sleep in laboratory animals in 1959, he began to investigate sleep mechanisms with electrophysiological and anatomical techniques. In the late sixties Jouvet and his co-workers focused their efforts on the role of neurotransmitters in sleep regulation. Using an impressive array of anatomical, physiological, pharmacological, and biochemical techniques, he carried out numerous basic experiments that laid the groundwork for a new theory of sleep regulation—the monamine theory.

In order to provide some impression of this research, I have selected one aspect for a more detailed description. The nuclei of nerve cells containing the neurotransmitter serotonin are located near the midline of the brainstem known as the raphe.

The axons of these nerve cells project upward into regions of the forebrain as well as downward into the spinal cord, where, by releasing serotonin, they affect other nerve cells. The finding that a destruction of raphe nuclei in laboratory animals led to a drastic reduction of sleep suggested that serotonin played a central role in sleep regulation. If this assumption was correct, then it ought to be possible to abolish sleep by inhibiting serotonin synthesis. Figure 8.2 shows that the synthesis of serotonin proceeds in two steps. Tryptophan, an amino acid that is a normal constituent of food, is transformed by the enzyme tryptophan-hydroxylase into 5-hydroxytryptophan, the immediate precursor of serotonin. It is possible to inhibit the action of this rate-limiting enzyme, by administering the substance parachlorophenylalanine (abbreviated PCPA). In laboratory animals PCPA was shown to inhibit serotonin synthesis and thereby disrupt the activity of serotonin-containing nerve cells. Jouvet and his co-workers, and the Swiss physiolo-

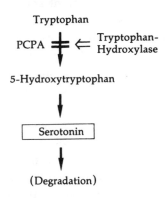

FIGURE 8.2
PCPA blocks the enzyme tryptophan-hydroxylase.
The neurotransmitter serotonin is synthesized in the human body from the amino acid tryptophan, which is present in food. The enzyme tryptophan-hydroxylase is necessary to transform tryptophan into 5-hydroxytrypto-phan, an intermediate step in the synthesis of serotonin. If this enzyme is blocked by the substance parachlorophenylalanine, which inhibits its effect, then serotonin can no longer be synthesized.

gist Werner Koella, who was then working in the United States, could show that injections of PCPA in animals led to prolonged sleeplessness. If these animals were given 5-hydroxytrypto- phan, their nerve cells could temporarily synthesize serotonin again, since the blocked step in the chain of synthesis had been circumvented. Injecting the immediate precursor of serotonin into PCPA-treated animals was shown to reinstate sleep for a short time.

These experiments confirmed the important role of serotonin in sleep regulation. They also suggested an interesting possibil- ity, namely, that insomniac patients might take tryptophan to increase their synthesis of serotonin and thus improve their sleep. Although a number of investigations of the sleep-pro- moting effects of tryptophan have been undertaken, in both animals and men (see chapter 5), the results have been largely disappointing. Although some authors reported a sleep-pro- moting action of tryptophan, the effect was weak and could not be confirmed in some of the studies. Recent results indicate that even drugs that specifically increase the activity of serotonin- containing nerve cells fail to enhance sleep. In light of these findings it is possible that the slight sleep-promoting effect which has been reported for high doses of tryptophan is not mediated by serotonin-containing nerve cells.

Up to now we have concentrated on the role of serotonin. However, the monoamine theory also takes into account the activity of the transmitters noradrenaline, dopamine, and ace- tylcholine. Without going into further detail, we should bear in mind the basic tenet of this theory: that sleep regulation occurs as a result of the balance and interaction of different neuro- transmitter systems. We will return to this subject at the end of the present chapter.

Does a REM Sleep Center Exist?

In the early sixties Jouvet observed that the destruction of certain groups of nerve cells in the pons (a part of the brain; see figure 8.1) caused REM sleep to disappear completely. On the basis of these and other findings, he concluded that the structures responsible for REM sleep must be located in these regions of the brainstem. Let us stop for a moment and recall the typical signs of REM sleep in cats. The EEG shows small and rapid waves, similar to those recorded in the waking state. The eyes move in the familiar, rapid fashion, and muscle tension has practically disappeared, apart from occasional twitches. The question now took the following form: Do these changes typical of REM sleep all derive from the same source, or are they determined by the activity of different nerve cell systems?

The remarkable results described below pointed to the second hypothesis. If certain nerve cells in the pons of laboratory animals were destroyed, REM sleep still occurred, but muscle tension remained high. Animals in these experiments exhibited a bizarre behavior during REM sleep: they raised their heads, appeared to pursue and even attack nonexistent objects, or retreated and showed signs of aggression or fear. It looked just as if the inhibition of muscle relaxation enabled these animals to "act out" their REM sleep. These dramatic findings may indicate that animals also have dreamlike experiences in REM sleep.

Let us now return to the neurotransmitters. According to the monoamine theory of sleep regulation, nerve cells containing serotonin trigger a REM sleep episode, while the systems containing noradrenaline and acetylcholine are responsible for the actual process of REM sleep. Allan Hobson and Robert McCarley, sleep researchers and psychiatrists at Harvard Medical School, further investigated this problem by studying in particular the role of the neurotransmitter acetylcholine. After implanting cannulae in the pons, they injected tiny amounts of

FIGURE 8.3
A Cat "Acts Out Its REM Sleep."
If certain nerve cells in the brainstem are destroyed, muscle activity during
REM sleep is no longer inhibited. The sleeping cat raises its head, gets up,
moves around, and appears to attack nonexistent objects. (From a film
sequence by Morrison, 1983.)

carbachol, a substance that imitates the effect of the transmitter acetylcholine but has a more prolonged action. The results of the injection were spectacular: the animals spent hours in a state very similar to that of REM sleep. These and related experiments led Hobson and McCarley to conclude that an interaction takes place between the cells containing acetylcholine on the one hand and those containing noradrenaline and serotonin on the other. Although it is not possible to go into detail here, these authors reached the conclusion that this interaction between the two cell groups is responsible for the generation of the non-REM/REM sleep cycle (described in chapter 2).

We have dealt chiefly with animal experiments so far, without asking the question, Do these results also apply to man? This appears to be so; the results do apply, at least as far as the transmitter acetylcholine is concerned. Two scientists at the National Institute of Mental Health, Christian Gillin and Natray Sitaram, conducted experiments on the influence of acetylcholine-like substances on the REM sleep of human subjects. Sleep was recorded in a sleep laboratory with the usual procedures, but in addition a cannula was placed in a vein of the arm, so that injections could be made from the next room while the participants were asleep. If the subjects were injected with arecoline, a substance with an effect similar to acetylcholine's, shortly after they had fallen asleep, REM sleep occurred very early in the night. But when, on other nights of the experiment, they were injected with the drug scopolamine, which blocks the effect of acetylcholine in the brain, REM sleep was considerably delayed. These results indicate that the transmitter acetylcholine plays an important role in REM sleep regulation of both animals and man. Another observation deserves mention in this context: Gillin and Sitaram noticed that arecoline injections produced an especially rapid onset of REM sleep in depressive patients. This finding prompted the hypothesis that depression might be accompanied by an oversensitivity of nerve cells to the transmitter acetylcholine, a phenomenon that could be of great significance not only for sleep but also for our understanding of this illness.

Contradictions and New Developments

The monoamine theory has stimulated sleep research to an extraordinary degree in the last ten years and permitted us to place a large number of different experimental results in a logical context. On the other hand, the most recent experiments have uncovered certain contradictions to the postulates of the theory as originally formulated. One example emerged from a test on rats, which showed that treatment with the inhibitor of serotonin synthesis, PCPA, caused only temporary sleeplessness, even though serotonin levels in the brain remained low for a long time. Apparently, adaptive mechanisms in the brain make it possible for sleep to occur despite the partial disruption of the serotonin system. Together with Irene Tobler I was able to demonstrate that although animals treated with PCPA sleep very little, they can nonetheless achieve, after a twenty-four-hour period of sleep deprivation, a percentage of deep sleep equal to that of control animals. These findings suggest that an important component of sleep regulation remains intact even if the concentration of serotonin in the brain has been greatly reduced. How can we explain these results? These contradictions to the monoamine theory (as well as others that have arisen) can probably be traced back to the fact that the transmitters involved in the regulation of sleep are also involved in the regulation of other brain functions. This is indicated by the behavior of a PCPA-treated animal, which will exhibit in addition to sleeplessness an increased sensitivity to pain and other external influences, as well as more aggression and intensified sexual behavior. It is thus conceivable that the sleep disturbance arises not from a direct interference with the sleep-regulating system but from changes in other brain functions. This brings us back to the fundamental question of whether it is possible to investigate sleep as an isolated phenomenon, or whether we must not agree with Walter Hess that the problem of sleep "cannot be solved on its own, but only in terms of an analysis of the entire functional structure of the organism."[3]

Doubts concerning the basic postulates of the monoamine theory have also arisen in another connection. In addition to the "classic" transmitters with which the theory concerns itself (noradrenaline, serotonin, acetylcholine, and so on), new discoveries about the functions of related substances are constantly being made. By 1981 twenty-five peptides (building blocks of protein molecules) were known to be present in the brain, some of which play a role similar to that of transmitters. Since then several more of these peptides have been found in the brain. Most recently, nerve cells have even been identified in which a "classic" transmitter occurs in combination with a peptide. This finding contradicts the long-held principle in brain research that only one type of transmitter is present at a synapse. Since this no longer appears to be true, the relatively simple "maps" of the brain based on the monoamines have grown increasingly intricate and complex, and as a result the functional framework becomes more and more puzzling. As we will see in the next chapter, evidence is accumulating that certain peptides play a central role in sleep regulation.

The history of brain research shows that it is not new ideas alone that lead to new discoveries but also the invention and application of new techniques. The recording of electrical signals was one of the most important new methods in experimental sleep research and in other areas of neurobiology, for investigating the relation between brain functions and behavior. It is much more difficult to continuously follow chemical changes in the brain, since a chemical analysis normally requires the removal of brain tissue. Whereas such procedures cannot reveal a process they may provide a "snapshot" of a momentary state. Raymond Cespuglio, a scientist at the University of Lyon, has introduced a new electrochemical recording method into sleep research. Special, fine electrodes are permanently implanted in certain regions of the brain, where they can register the local concentration of neurotransmitters in sleeping and waking animals. This technique has brought us one step closer to a "chemical EEG," which makes it possible to record chemical processes in the brain continuously, as they are taking place, and to study their relationship to the sleep/wake cycle. We should soon be in a position to know whether this procedure will provide fundamental new insights into the chemical regulation of sleep. The recognition of the complex chemical organization of the brain has prompted many scientists to assign a higher priority to the basic physiological principles: thus sleep is being regarded more and more as a biological process governed by certain rules; these rules need to be studied even if the details of the underlying mechanisms are not yet understood. Sleep deprivation has proved to be an extremely useful tool in the study of the processes involved in sleep regulation. This approach has led to several theoretical models that will be the subject of the last chapter. However, besides these physiological approaches to the problem, we are also experiencing a revival of old chemical theories that date back as far as the beginning of this century. These theories focus on the question of endogenous sleep substances (that is, ones produced naturally by the human body itself), and it is to this subject that the next chapter is devoted.

9

The Search for
Endogenous
Sleep Substances

Our studies have established that the accumulation of the
hypnotoxin produces an increasing need for sleep.
—Henri Piéron
Le Probléme Physiologique du Sommeil (1913)

"Scientists find substance that causes natural sleep!"

"The stuff of which dreams are made may be available in
capsule form within a few years!"

"Silent revolution on the sleeping pill market!"

"Sleep from a test tube!"

These and other, similar headlines, reporting alleged sensational discoveries of natural, endogenous sleep substances, crop
up every now and again in the newspapers. Most readers probably find it difficult to get a clear picture of what such reports
really mean. Does the human body actually produce substances
that cause sleep?

Until a few years ago this possibility was not regarded seriously by most of the experts. Little notice was taken of the few
scientists who were testing this hypothesis in experiments.

They were too far off the main track of neurobiological research, and so it tended to be an unusual type of researcher who chose to work in the field of endogenous sleep substances. They were people who did not mind being outsiders and who were prepared to pursue their offbeat ideas for years or even decades with patience and persistence. Since they were not carried along on any wave of fashionable trends, like many of their colleagues, their work received little support or attention. Many people wondered whether these scientists were misguided cranks or in fact pioneering geniuses.

In the mid-1970s the situation took a new turn. A young Scottish scientist made a totally unexpected discovery: he established the existence in the brain of a new class of endogenous, pain-relieving substances that have an effect similar to that of the well-known painkillers opium and morphine. They were given the names enkephalins and endorphins and belong to the chemical group of peptides, which are components of proteins. A decade ago the idea that the brain might contain endogenous opiates would have been dismissed as a strange and most unlikely speculation; in those days brain functions like sleep and pain were studied almost exclusively in the context of changes in the neurotransmitters. In the meantime, however, various peptides have been discovered that function similarly to transmitters or hormones. Their relationship to the well-known, "classic" neurotransmitters has become the subject of intensive research. This new development placed in question many theories that had previously appeared to be firmly grounded and established. One of its most positive results was to remind scientists of the extent of their ignorance. The scientific community has since become more receptive to unconventional approaches. Nowadays the idea that specific endogenous substances could play a part in sleep regulation is no longer dismissed as a flight of fancy, but is being seriously discussed by leading sleep experts.

The Early Experiments of Piéron

"If the waking state is maintained over a long period of time, then the need for sleep becomes more and more powerful, until it finally becomes irresistible. This phenomenon takes place in conjunction with poisoning by a hypothetical substance, which has the characteristics of toxins . . ."[1] This passage is taken from *Le problème physiologique du sommeil* (The Physiological Problem of Sleep), a book published by the French physiologist Henri Piéron in 1913. In it Piéron formulated the hypothesis that in the course of our waking hours a "sleep poison" (hypnotoxin) accumulates in our bodies and causes an increasing desire to sleep. As we sleep, our bodies break this substance down chemically and eliminate it. As a way of testing his theory, Piéron conducted experiments with dogs. He kept them awake during the daytime and prevented them from sleeping at night by taking them for walks through the streets of Paris. Then he removed some cerebrospinal fluid (the liquid that fills the cavities of the brain) from these dogs and injected it into animals that had been allowed to rest normally. He observed that the dogs that received these injections reacted by falling asleep, and he considered this to be a confirmation of his hypothesis.

Piéron's findings do not look very impressive in the light of present-day knowledge, particularly from a technical standpoint: the then-existing techniques for removing and injecting the cerebrospinal fluid probably involved considerable stress on the animals and thus affected their behavior. In spite of such reservations, however, Piéron must be credited with a major achievement: he was the first to propose an explicit neurochemical theory of sleep regulation and to test it in experiments.

Factor S and SPS: Are They Modern "Hypnotoxins"?

Piéron's work became widely known in the early decades of this century, but only one research group actually made an effort to test his theories. In 1939 two American scientists, J. G. Schnedorf and A. C. Ivy, published their results confirming Piéron's findings in large measure.

Then, in the mid-1960s, John Pappenheimer, a professor of physiology at Harvard Medical School, began a series of experiments designed to probe further into the subject of endogenous sleep substances. In his previous research work Pappenheimer had specialized in the physiology of brain fluid circulation and had developed a technique for permanently implanting small hollow needles in the brains of goats. He was then able to remove cerebrospinal fluid without putting the laboratory animals under severe stress. Goats offered the advantage, for this experiment, of their relatively large size and the correspondingly large amount of fluid that could be obtained from their brains. Pappenheimer and his associates prevented the goats from sleeping for two or three days, and at different points during this period of sleep deprivation they removed brain fluid. This fluid was then injected into the brain cavities of rats that had also been provided with permanently implanted cannulae. Rats were chosen as recipients because, thanks to their small size, they needed to be injected with only small amounts of fluid. The test showed that rats that had been injected with the brain fluid from sleep-deprived goats slept more than control rats that had received fluid from nondeprived goats.

These first results appeared to support the hypnotoxin theory. The next question to arise concerned the chemical structure of this sleep substance. Pappenheimer named it factor S (S for "sleep"). The search for its structure began, and would involve a long series of experiments lasting fifteen years. James Krueger, a young biochemist, was responsible for the chemical part of the research project. The brain fluid of the donor animals was separated by chemical means into several fractions, each containing various substances. Then, one by one, each of these fractions was tested to see whether it had a sleep-inducing effect, in order to identify the fraction containing factor S. This tedious procedure was repeated several times, until the unknown sleep substance gradually became more concentrated in the solution. Soon it became evident that the amounts of brain fluid available would not be sufficient to isolate factor S, since it was present in such extraordinarily small quantities. Pappenheimer and his co-workers began using cattle brains obtained from slaughterhouses. As recipients for the injections, they selected rabbits, which proved to be more suitable for this type of experiment than did rats, since their sleep shows less variability from animal to animal. It could be shown that the fractions containing a more concentrated amount of factor S increased the percentage of non-REM sleep and caused large, slow EEG waves to appear. (Rabbits have very little REM sleep.) The EEG pattern was very similar to the one that typically appears after sleep deprivation. The sleep-promoting effect of factor S lasted for several hours and showed all the signs of natural sleep.

The fact remained, however, that the sleep substance still had not been isolated, and it became clear once again that the quantity of available brain material would not be sufficient for the task. Pappenheimer and his associates solved this problem in a highly original manner. Since they had realized in the meantime that the sleep substance is chemically very stable, they concluded that most of the factor S in the body must be eliminated in urine. In contrast to brain tissue, urine is available in almost any desired quantity. They used as a starting point large amounts of human urine that had been collected for another medical purpose, and they were able to demonstrate the presence of the sleep substance. From this point on, things moved rapidly, and the substance could be chemically isolated. By

1981 the active principle of factor S was known, although the final details of its chemical structure (sequential analysis) were still lacking. Factor S turned out to be a relatively small peptide, consisting of five amino acids. Most unexpectedly, muramic acid was one of them. It was known to occur in the cell membranes of bacteria, but until then it had not been found in higher organisms. A compound of muramic acid, muramyl-dipeptide (MDP), has been known to immunologists for some time as a compound that stimulates an organism's defensive reaction to foreign substances and causes fever. Krueger and Pappenheimer were able to demonstrate that MDP also induces sleep in rabbits. The success of this research should not mislead anyone into thinking that all questions have been answered, for a number of important problems remain to be solved. First, the sleep substance needs to be synthesized so that it becomes available in larger quantity. When this has been achieved, it will be important to test and confirm the sleep-inducing effect in more laboratory experiments. Another question that must be answered is whether different animal species react to the substance in the same way. Up to now Pappenheimer and his associates have reported positive findings with rats, cats, rabbits, and monkeys.

Leaving the American continent, we turn to a similar and equally interesting project in Asia. In the mid-1970s a Japanese research team began a systematic investigation of the hypnotoxin theory by means of the most modern techniques. The head of the team, Koji Uchizono, is a noted physiologist and director of the large National Institute for Medical Research in Japan. Shojiro Inoué, a biocyberneticist and professor at the outstanding School of Medicine and Dentistry at the University of Tokyo, took charge of the animal experiments in collaboration with Hiroaki Nagasaki. Yasuo Komoda, a biochemist, undertook the chemical side of the project. The experimental approach resembled that of Pappenheimer's group: rats were deprived of sleep for one day and then killed; their brains provided the material from which the group attempted to isolate sleep-inducing substances. Professor Inoué and his co-worker Kazuki Honda had developed an extremely sensitive method for investigating the sleep-promoting effects of fractions of cerebrospinal fluid. The recipients of the injections (also rats) were not only provided with the usual brain and muscle electrodes for recording sleep but also were implanted permanently with small hollow needles, by means of which liquid could be continuously infused into their brain cavities. This infusion consisted either of the chemical fraction under investigation or of an inactive control solution. In order to reduce the influence of other factors to a minimum, the animals were kept in an environment with a constant temperature and an artificial light/dark cycle. Using this procedure, the team could show that a substance present in the brains of the sleep-deprived donor animals could promote sleep in the recipients. They named it SPS, for sleep-promoting substance. Their experiments showed that the effects of SPS persisted for up to twenty-four hours after the infusion and that the effect was influenced by the phase of the light/dark cycle. The chemical structure of SPS is still unknown.

My research group at the University of Zurich also found indications that sleep-inducing substances are present in the brain fluid of rats. In the midseventies I was able to show, in experiments undertaken with two medical students, Josef Sachs and Jan Ungar, that the cerebrospinal fluid of donor animals can alter the motor activity of the recipients. If the fluid was removed from the donor animals during the active phase of their daily rhythm, the activity of the recipients was increased. On the other hand, fluid taken from inactive or resting animals led, when injected into recipients, to a decrease in activity. In later studies made in association with Irene Tobler, small amounts of cerebrospinal fluid from sleep-deprived rats when injected into the brain cavities of normal rats were observed to increase sleep. In order for the active substances to be identified, these preliminary experiments would have had to be followed by extensive tests.

DSIP—A Sleep Substance?

In the early sixties Marcel Monnier, a professor of physiology at the University of Basel, also set out to look for endogenous sleep substances. As it happened, this project would occupy him for twenty years. Monnier had been a student of Walter Hess, the Zurich professor of medicine and Nobel Prize winner. It was mentioned in the preceding chapter that Hess had been able to show how electrical brain stimulation leads to sleep. Monnier used this procedure to put rabbits to sleep. He built on Piéron's findings as well, proceeding on the assumption that the electrical stimulation of the brain releases a sleep substance that ought to be identifiable in the bloodstream. With the help of two young medical students, Theodor Koller (who is today a professor of cell biology at the Federal Institute of Technology in Zurich) and Luzius Hösli (now a professor of physiology in Basel), he developed a technique for removing blood from sleeping animals and isolating a particular part of the plasma, which might contain the sleep substance, with the aid of a semipermeable membrane. When this blood fraction was injected into normal animals, it put them to sleep. Like Pappenheimer, Monnier was assisted in the later stages of his research by a chemist, Guido Schoenenberger, who purified and identified the active substance. He was able to show in the end that the electrical brain stimulation releases a peptide consisting of nine amino acids. This substance was named delta-sleep-inducing peptide (DSIP), because it promoted mainly sleep with slow EEG waves (delta waves). Once the exact chemical structure of DSIP had been established, this peptide could be synthesized in the chemical laboratory without major difficulty. According to Monnier and Schoenenberger, no observable difference exists between the effects of the natural and the synthetic products.

Since DSIP became commercially available, various research teams have studied its biological effects. However, the published reports yield no clear picture of the properties of this substance. Not all the research groups could confirm that DSIP actually induces sleep. In some careful studies no effect at all could be observed. In other experiments positive results were obtained, but the impact on sleep stages varied in different animal species. Whereas in rabbits an increase in slow-wave sleep (delta sleep) was observed, in cats it was REM sleep that was enhanced. Reports on the first tests involving intravenous DSIP injections in man described a positive effect, which did not occur, however, until several hours after the peptide had been administered.

Not only is it difficult to interpret the effect of DSIP on sleep, but the picture is further confused by other puzzling findings. It is not clear, for example, why DSIP can be found in other organs besides the brain (liver, lungs, intestines), nor is it yet understood how injections of this peptide can influence the regulation of body temperature. On the basis of these varied results, Schoenenberger has come to the conclusion that DSIP is not a specific sleep substance but rather a "programmer" of rhythmic processes. However, this conclusion is not yet supported by much hard data. It may be important to bear in mind that the isolation of DSIP proceeded from electrical stimulation of the brain. Brain stimulation may well induce effects other than sleep, and this may help account for the variety of phenomena that have been observed in connection with this peptide. More experiments are needed to clarify the biological effects of DSIP.

Does a REM Sleep Substance Exist?

The putative sleep substances that have been mentioned so far —factor S, SPS, and DSIP—appear primarily to increase the percentage of the deep stages of non-REM sleep. Are there any substances specifically connected with the regulation of REM sleep? The most extensive studies on this problem have been made by the Mexican sleep researcher Raoul Drucker-Colin. In the 1960s he began a series of experiments with cats, in which he permanently implanted two hollow needles in their brains and irrigated the tissue of the brainstem between the needles with a small amount of liquid. He observed that after a REM sleep episode the liquid flowing out of the brain contained an increased amount of protein.

If, before beginning the experiment, he treated the animals with substances that block protein synthesis in the brain, no REM sleep occurred at all. These results suggested that during REM sleep episodes certain proteins are released in the brainstem, substances that have not yet been identified but that could be involved in the regulation of this sleep stage. In recent years Drucker-Colin has made use of new immunological techniques to try to shed more light on this problem. He was able to show that the injection of antibodies raised against the protein fraction reduces REM sleep. However, REM sleep can be suppressed by a large variety of influences, and so it is not yet clear whether Drucker-Colin's substances play a specific role.

Other indications of the existence of endogenous substances that regulate REM sleep have come from Jouvet's laboratory in Lyon. In these experiments animals were deprived of REM sleep, and cerebrospinal fluid was then removed from their brain cavity. Other animals were treated with the substance PCPA (the inhibitor of serotonin synthesis), a procedure that suppressed their REM sleep almost entirely. When this second group of animals was injected with the brain fluid of the first donor group, the fluid was able to reverse the PCPA-induced REM sleep suppression. Clearly a REM-sleep-promoting substance was present in the cerebrospinal fluid of donor animals.

It is important to note that all of these results are still preliminary and inconclusive; they cannot yet be regarded as firm evidence that specific substances are actually responsible for the regulation of REM sleep.

Other Possible Sleep Substances

A whole list of endogenous substances have been observed to possess sleep-promoting effects. Only a few of them can be mentioned here. The pineal gland is located in the brain, tucked away between the two hemispheres. Its function is still largely unknown. This gland releases the hormone melatonin, whose concentration is particularly high during the night. Experiments conducted in animals and man have shown that melatonin may promote sleep. This problem was recently investigated in a collaborative study with Josephine Arendt, an English bio-chemist. In these experiments volunteers were given small doses of melatonin every afternoon for one month. This treatment induced a strong urge to sleep in the early hours of the evening. In this instance, too, further research will be necessary to determine whether the hormone had a direct influence on sleep or whether it affected sleep indirectly by phase-shifting circadian rhythm.

Another hormone has received a great deal of attention in recent years: arginine vasotocin (AVT). In 1977 a Romanian research group published a report stating that the injection of extremely small amounts of AVT (only 600 molecules) into the brain cavities of cats induced sleep. Although these results were not confirmed by other researchers, human experiments have already been conducted in Romania, where the substance was given to adolescents and even to young children. Once again a sleep-promoting effect was reported, consisting mainly of an increase in REM sleep. Since such human experiments are eth-ically unacceptable in most countries, it is difficult to evaluate these findings. Finally, another example of a possible sleep sub-stance emerged from the work of Françoise Riou, Raymond Cespuglio, and Michel Jouvet in Lyon, who recently reported the sleep-promoting effect of "vasoactive intestinal polypep-tide" (VIP). This is a peptide consisting of several amino acids; it occurs in the human body and affects blood vessels and the intestines, among other organs. VIP was discovered in the brain only recently. The research group in Lyon found that injections of VIP in the brain cavities of rats increased their sleep (particularly REM sleep during the light phase of their twenty-four-hour daily cycle).

New Developments and Conclusions

The work of Shojiro Inoué and James Krueger has already been described. Most recently these scientists have begun to follow up new clues. In 1983 Inoué and his co-workers, in collaboration with a research team from the University of Kyoto, discovered that prostaglandin D2 induces sleep when minute amounts of it are injected into the brains of rats. Prostaglandins are endogenous substances that play an important role in the process of inflammation and are also involved in the generation of fever. Medications like aspirin, for instance, which are used to combat inflammation and fever, work by preventing the synthesis of prostaglandins. Various prostaglandins exist, some of which have been studied more thoroughly than others. In particular, very little is known about the function of prostaglandin D2, even though this form is particularly abundant in the rat brain. The research group of Ryuji Ueno and Osamu Hayaishi in Kyoto discovered the sleep-promoting effect of this substance by serendipity but then confirmed the effect by careful experiments. One of the exciting aspects of this discovery is the fact that the amount of prostaglandin D2 needed to induce sleep corresponds quite closely to its natural concentration in brain tissue. This means that no high "pharmacological" doses are necessary to produce an effect; it also suggests that the variations in the concentration of prostaglandin D2 that occur naturally in the brain may play a role in the regulation of sleep.

A further piece of evidence suggests a connection between the body's defense reactions (immune responses), which are activated, for example, by inflammation, and sleep. Interleukins belong to a group of substances released by white blood cells and probably involved in defending the body against invading microorganisms. Adriano Fontana, an immunologist in Zurich, and his co-workers have demonstrated that interleukin is also synthesized in cultures of certain brain cells. It is clear that this substance performs some function in the brain, although this function has not yet been identified in any detail. Krueger recently reported that the injection of tiny amounts of Interleukin-1 into the brain cavities of rabbits causes them to fall asleep within a few minutes. A striking aspect of these findings is the time factor: the interval between the injection and the onset of sleep is significantly shorter than in the case of factor S or prostaglandin D2. The minimal sleep-inducing amount of Interleukin-1 is based only on estimates as yet, since its chemical structure has not been identified, but it appears to be smaller than that of all other substances tested so far. (Vasotocin might be an exception, but these findings are still unconfirmed.) Although the first results are exciting, we must wait for further information before we can assess the general significance of these discoveries.

As we have already seen, the currently available sleep medications are far from ideal. One of the limitations of such hypnotic agents is revealed by a detailed investigation of the sleep EEG: the sleep induced by drugs is not the same as natural sleep. The medical treatment of sleep disturbances would take a giant step forward if natural, endogenous substances could be used. It is conceivable that some forms of sleep disorder arise from a lack of such substances in the body and that one could cure sleep disorders by providing the substances to the organism from outside sources. An analogous form of "substitution therapy" is being successfully used for diabetes: the hormone insulin, which the pancreas of diabetics produces in insufficient amounts, can be provided by means of injections. As far as the treatment of sleep disorders is concerned, such forms of therapy still lie in the future. They will not become a practical reality until further progress is made; the sleep substances must be chemically isolated and their mechanisms clarified before they can be used in medical therapy.

By way of conclusion we should recall to mind the various "research philosophies" that underlie the studies and experiments described in this chapter. It was Piéron's concept of a hypnotoxin that broke the ground for the later experiments leading to the discoveries of factor S, SPS, and DSIP. All of these research projects were based on the assumption that the urge to sleep has a chemical origin. The sleep pressure was heightened by means of sleep deprivation or, in some cases—possibly less specifically—by electrical brain stimulation. This approach required no assumptions or prior information about the nature of the unknown substance. It was eventually identified by obtaining successively purer chemical fractions of the original material. This concept of research, which we might call agnostic, stands in contrast to the type that proceeds from a basis of already available neurobiological knowledge. The monoamine theory discussed in chapter 8 is a good example of this second type of approach. It used findings in anatomy, physiology, and pharmacology to assign to neurotransmitter systems a central role in sleep regulation. The last two decades of research have revealed a problem in this type of approach: as our knowledge of neurobiology continues to expand, a theory of this kind must constantly be adapted and reformulated to accommodate the newest discoveries. Such continual changes may impair a theory's basic plausibility.

A further approach consisted of testing, by the trial-and-error method, already known endogenous substances for their possible effect on sleep. (The link between VIP and sleep emerged in this fashion.) Or, as happened with prostaglandin D2, its sleep-inducing effect was discovered by accident. If experiments of this kind happen to produce positive results, explanations must be sought after the fact by means of physiological tests. This procedure is reminiscent of the discovery of the sleep medications we have today, most of which were found through trial and error or accidentally. Whichever path is chosen in the search for new substances, the most important factor will remain the confirmation of a substance's effectiveness, for in the final analysis nothing succeeds like success.

10

Sleep Deprivation

... let the doctors determine whether sleep is so necessary
that life depends on it. For we certainly find that they put
to death King Perseus of Macedonia, when he was a pris-
oner in Rome, by preventing him from sleeping; but Pliny
instances people who lived a long time without sleep.
—MICHEL DE MONTAIGNE
Essays

The topic of this chapter is of importance for both basic and
applied scientific research; outside the bounds of science, the
idea of going without sleep arises in interesting connections
throughout the history of human culture. For modern researchers experiments with sleep deprivation provide important insights into the regulatory mechanism and functions of sleep,
but more practically oriented research can also profit from tests
of this kind.

Let us begin by considering some of the effects of sleep deprivation on various sectors of the working population. It can lead
to a reduction of a person's ability to function effectively; this
can have disastrous consequences for car drivers or for indus-
trial workers. People who have to work on shifts and sleep at
unaccustomed times may easily accumulate a chronic sleep
deficit. The effects of insufficient sleep are also of interest to the
military, since soldiers sometimes have to get along on little
sleep for long periods. This can reduce their capacity to carry
out orders, to judge situations correctly, or to make decisions,
and it may lessen their motivation in general.

Sometimes sleep deprivation is caused intentionally. American pilots captured by the Chinese in the Korean War were subjected to a form of brainwashing in which they were prevented from sleeping as one way of breaking down their resistance. Such methods are not new. The Swiss psychologist Hermann Huber-Weidmann has written on the *tormentum vigiliae* (waking torture) in use among the ancient Romans. The *tortura insomniae* (insomnia torture), which was widely practiced in the Middle Ages, was designed not only to force confessions from prisoners but also to drive out demons. In the eighteenth century the German Lutheran theologian Christian Thomasius condemned these practices in his treatise *On the Right to Sleep and Dream.* It thus appears somewhat paradoxical that sleep deprivation, often misused as a form of torture, has been discovered by modern medicine in the last ten years as a form of treatment for depressive patients. We will return to this new type of therapy later in another context.

The most widely differing cultures have viewed an overcoming of the urge to sleep as a desirable, though very difficult, goal. Mircea Eliade, a well-known scholar of comparative religions, has written on Australian tribes that do not permit young men to sleep for three nights during initiation rites. The hero of Mesopotamian legends Gilgamesh is supposed to have been given the task of going without sleep for six days and nights in his strivings to become immortal. Since sleep overcame him in spite of all his efforts, he was obliged to remain among mortals. In his book *Visions* the theologian Ernst Benz mentions several examples of ascetic vigils that were intended to make the waker more receptive to spiritual experiences. One case in point was the religious services—called pannichides—of the early Christian monks, which lasted all night. The rituals of monasteries in the Eastern churches do not permit the participants to sleep more than three or four hours at a time, since the night service does not end until after midnight and the morning service begins at four.

Many great ascetic philosophers have praised the struggle

against sleep because they regarded the time spent asleep as lost or wasted. To help them achieve their goal, they used stones for pillows. Peter of Alcántara, who sat resting his head against a post, allegedly never slept for more than an hour and a half a day for forty years. At the end of the eighteenth century the German poet and mystic Novalis praised sleeplessness, observing that "the less sleep we need, the more closely we approach perfection."[1]

Experimental Sleep Deprivation

In 1896 G. Patrick and J. Gilbert, two scientists working at the Psychology Laboratory of the University of Iowa, published their report on the effects of a ninety-hour period of sleep deprivation on three healthy young men. This first scientific study was to be followed by many others. One of the participants was a twenty-eight-year-old assistant professor at the university. During his ninety hours without sleep, he tried to go about his normal business as far as possible in the daytime; he spent the nights in reading and playing games at the beginning, and in more energetic activities like going for walks in the later phases of the experiment. Periodically the participants were tested on their ability to perform tasks and were subjected to various physiological recordings. The authors of this study reported that the first night passed with relatively few problems but that the second night was marked by a strong urge to sleep. In the second half of the experiment one subject could no longer sit down idle, since he would immediately fall asleep despite the greatest efforts of willpower. From the second night on, illusions and disturbances of perception began to occur, and the subject complained that the floor was covered with a layer of sticky, moving particles that made it hard for him to walk. Still later he reported that the air was filled with colored specks. These sensory illusions disappeared completely once the subject had been allowed to sleep again for ten and a half hours after the termination of the experiment. The other two subjects in this study experienced no disturbances of perception during their sleep deprivation, but they also had great difficulty in staying awake. They, too, felt completely rested after they were able to sleep for an extended period.

The World Record

Three series of experiments took place in the 1960s in which participants remained awake from seven to nine days under controlled laboratory conditions and observation. In 1965 Randy Gardner, a seventeen-year-old California college student, decided to try for a new world record. He spent most of the time during the attempt in the company of two friends, who managed—with considerable difficulty—to keep him awake for several days. For the last ninety hours of the experiment, the sleep expert William Dement and his associates took over the task of keeping Randy under observation. Although he showed some signs of lack of sleep, they were surprisingly small. After four or five days the young man became irritable and suspicious. He began to report daydreams and exhibited some memory loss. During one walk at night he had definite sensory disturbances. Dement describes how hard it was, especially at night, to keep the young man from sleeping, for his eyelids had become heavy and painful and he had begun to lose his motivation for the whole experiment. He found it easier to stay awake in the daytime. Toward the end the press and television crews began covering the experiment, and this naturally increased Randy's motivation again. After eleven days the hour had come: Randy held a last press conference, at which he managed to cut an excellent figure. According to Dement, when he was asked how he had been able to set this world record, he answered, "It's just mind over matter." After exactly 264 hours and 12 minutes without sleeping, he fell into a deep sleep in the sleep laboratory of the San Diego Naval Hospital and slept for 14 hours and 40 minutes; when he woke up, he was practically recovered.

State of Health and Performance Levels during Sleep Deprivation

According to Dement, Randy Gardner's world record demonstrates that it is possible for people to undergo long periods of sleep deprivation without serious impairment of mental functions. He does emphasize, however, that several factors were important for Randy's success: his excellent physical condition, his strong motivation, and the support he received from the supervisors of the experiment and from the media. Many other tests on sleep loss have resulted in much more severe disturbance in the participants. Hermann Huber-Weidmann has collected some of these findings in his book *Sleep, Sleep Disturbances, and Sleep Deprivation*. [2]

Let us now follow such a typical experiment. The first night usually presents no problem. If the experiment is taking place in a group, as is often the case, the first phase is typically marked by a relaxed and cheerful mood. The participants approach the test as if it were a contest or sporting event they want to win, and in this early phase they exhibit cooperative behavior and initiative. The positive mood carries on into the second day. In the second night the test subjects have more trouble staying awake, and the hours between 3 and 5 A.M. are critical: the urge to sleep appears impossible to resist. If the participants are given long test problems to solve, they invariably fall asleep but immediately deny having fallen asleep when the experimenter arouses them. On the next day the cheerful atmosphere has obviously vanished. The subjects are serious, tense, and lacking in enthusiasm for the tasks they are given to perform. They grow increasingly indifferent and apathetic and react irritably to being disturbed. Although they are still willing to follow the instructions of the experimenter, they show no initiative. Strong swings in mood can often be observed in this phase, as when an irritable temper suddenly shifts to overexcited activity. The subjects are not capable of undergoing a third sleepless night without help. To prevent them from falling asleep, the experimenter must constantly find new activities to keep them busy. Staying on their feet, doing gymnastic exercises, and going for walks are often the only effective techniques. In these late stages of sleep deprivation, the early hours of the morning are again the most difficult. Once this critical period has passed, the urge to sleep grows weaker again. From the third night on, so-called microsleep periods can often be observed. The participant stops whatever he or she is doing and stares into space for one to three seconds. (In later stages this can occur for up to six seconds.) During this brief period the EEG shows changes typical of sleep. The end of a microsleep period is accompanied by a feeling of returning to full awareness. In this stage, disturbances of perception occur frequently. It appears that the borderline between sleeping and waking has become blurred, so that the kind of hallucinations that often occur at the moment of falling asleep now begin to invade the waking state as well. Both illusions (incorrect perception of existing objects) and actual hallucinations (perception of nonexistent objects) can be experienced in this stage. The surface of objects begins to waver; the floor appears to be covered with spiderwebs; faces appear and disappear. Auditory illusions also occur: a participant hears voices in the sound of a running water faucet and thinks they are talking about him. One tactile sensation that has been described repeatedly is the "hat phenomenon": the subject feels a ring of pressure around the forehead, as if he were wearing a hat.

When sleep deprivation experiments last more than four days, delusions can manifest themselves, in addition to the disturbances of perception. The participants grow increasingly suspicious and begin to believe that things are going on behind their backs that they are not being told about. One subject thought, after staying awake for four days, that the experimenters had slipped a drug into his coffee. In another test one participant became convinced that the supervisors wanted to kill him. He telephoned his wife and asked her to call the police. Finally, long-term sleep deprivation may give rise to symptoms of depersonalization, where the subject loses a clear sense of his own identity and can no longer relate to the normal world. Such severe psychic disturbances can be termed an actual sleep deprivation psychosis.

It is interesting to observe that these striking psychological alterations do not have corresponding physical symptoms. A sensation of burning and pain in the eyes and eyelids, as well as double vision, occurs relatively early. Pains in the limbs, a slight tremor, and impaired sensation in the arms and legs are occasionally reported. However, in spite of intensive efforts, no clear evidence of changes in metabolic activity caused by sleep deprivation has been found.

For obvious reasons a number of such sleep loss experiments were aimed mainly at observing the subjects' performance levels and abilities to function, which were measured in different tests. In the longer experiments the loss of performance ability was caused to a large degree by the loss of motivation and the increased occurrence of microsleep episodes. Microsleep is a particular problem when subjects are asked to perform tasks requiring concentration over an extended period of time. The American sleep researcher Harold Williams and his associates conducted a study in which the subjects were seated in front of a monitor for ten minutes and a different letter was flashed on the screen every second. The subjects were instructed to press a button every time the letter x appeared; the frequency of x was about one in every four letters. Before the experiment started, the participants were able to perform this simple task with virtually no errors, but after three days without sleep they failed to react to 25 percent of the x's shown; conversely, they often pressed the button for other letters. Microsleep episodes were without doubt the main cause for this drop in performance level.

The results of this experiment have a practical significance, since such "nodding off" for a second or two is a well-known and dangerous phenomenon in overtired car drivers. The drop in functional ability is pronounced in situations where concentration is required for an extended period of time. On the other hand, it is amazing to see how well sleep-deprived persons perform tasks needing only brief concentration. It is also surprising to see—as tests have repeatedly shown—that a single sleep period is sufficient to remove all traces of sleep-related psychological disturbances and performance deficits. The persistence of such problems has been reported only in a few individual cases. Psychotic personality changes continued to exist only very rarely after the end of an experiment, and in these cases it can be assumed that the subjects had a preexisting tendency to such disorders, which were merely triggered by the stressful procedure of sleep deprivation.

Can We Train Ourselves to Go without Sleep?

Like the religious ascetics of medieval times, many people today regard sleep as "time lost." They regret that the day is only twenty-four hours long and that they do not have time to do all the things they should do or would like to do. Wouldn't it be wonderful if that "wasted" third of our life could be used for other activities! We have already seen that some short sleepers exist who come close to this ideal. But what about the majority of normal people? Could they learn to reduce the amount of time they spend asleep?

Laverne Johnson's team in California pursued this question several years ago. Four young couples participated in an experiment. Three of them normally slept eight hours a night, while the fourth reported a normal sleep duration of only six and a half hours. The participants were given the task of gradually limiting their sleep to five and a half hours or less, by going to bed half an hour later every two to three weeks. After reaching their shortest sleeping time by this procedure, they were to remain at this sleep level for a month and then to reduce their sleep by a further thirty minutes for the next two months. The three couples who normally slept for eight hours were able to reduce their nightly sleep to five and a half, five, and four and a half hours respectively. The couple who normally slept for six and a half hours reduced their sleep to five hours. For the last six months of the experiment the participants were allowed to decide for themselves how long they wanted to sleep. Interestingly enough, all three of the couples who had previously slept a normal eight hours chose to maintain a sleep level significantly below their starting point (5.5 to 7.3 hours, an average of 6.4 hours). This study shows that it is possible for ordinary people to carry out an intentional reduction of their sleep by one to two hours over an extended period of time. A similar test conducted earlier by the same group produced comparable results.

How did the participants in this experiment feel? The couples who usually slept for eight hours had trouble getting up after less than six and a half hours of sleep, and complained of feeling tired. As their sleep was further reduced, they overslept more often in the mornings and had a stronger urge to take naps during the day. Overtiredness was finally the main reason why the participants did not reduce their sleep still further. Their performance levels, which were registered with various tests, were not significantly affected by the reduction in sleep.

A more recent study by the American sleep researchers Mary Carskadon and William Dement made clear that a reduction of sleep from the usual seven to nine hours to five hours increased the subjects' sleep propensity during the day. The effect of this cumulative sleep deficit disappeared entirely after the first ten-hour recovery sleep period.

Are We Chronically Sleep Deprived?

This question was the provocative title of a study published in 1975 by the American sleep researchers Wilse Webb and Harman Agnew. It has already been mentioned that most people would prefer to sleep an hour longer than they usually do. Recordings of rest/activity behavior confirm that many people actually do sleep longer on weekends. Is this extra sleep on Saturday and Sunday mornings a making up of a sleep deficit that we incur during the week? Or is it merely a pleasant luxury without any practical significance, which we could just as well do without?

The information available at this time does not provide clear answers to these questions, but a recently published study by Carskadon and Dement offers a few hints. These scientists have been interested in the question of daytime sleepiness for a number of years. One of their principal methods for measuring sleepiness consists of the "multiple sleep latency test," which their test subjects take at two-hour intervals from morning to evening. The subjects lie down in a darkened room and try to fall asleep. As soon as EEG and EMG recordings indicate the first signs of sleep, they are awakened. The test lasts a maximum of twenty minutes; if the subjects have not fallen asleep by that time, it is terminated. The time from lying down until falling asleep (that is, the sleep latency) is used as the measure of daytime sleep propensity. As figure 10.1 shows, the sleep latency is drastically reduced after one sleepless night. But it is also interesting to see that sleep latency increases (that is, sleepiness decreases) if the subject slept three to four hours longer than usual in the preceding night. These results lend support to the assumption that our normal amount of sleep lies below the ideal. It must be noted, however, that the study by Carskadon and Dement was conducted with college students, who are not necessarily representative of the whole population.

In this connection another practical aspect of longer sleep on

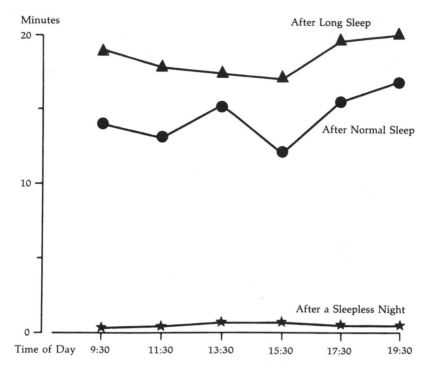

FIGURE 10.1
Time Required to Fall Asleep.

Repeated attempts to fall asleep during the day, after long sleep, normal sleep, and a sleepless night. The subjects lie down at two-hour intervals between 9:30 A.M. and 7:30 P.M. If they fall asleep, they are immediately awakened. The amount of time required to fall asleep is used as a measure of sleep propensity. After an extended sleep during the preceding night, the participants take a longer time to fall asleep; after a night without sleep, the time is greatly reduced. The points illustrated represent average values.

SOURCE: Adapted from M. Carskadon and W. Dement, "Current Perspectives on Daytime Sleepiness," *Sleep* 5, suppl. 2 (1982):73–81. Reprinted by permission of Raven Press, Publishers, New York.

weekends must be mentioned: if we extend our sleep on one night much beyond the norm, we may have trouble falling asleep on the next night, an observation that people who like to "sleep in" on Sunday mornings will find familiar. Since most people have trouble going to sleep before their usual bedtime, but must get up on weekdays at the time dictated by their job or family, they cannot maintain their ideal sleep levels. For this reason they have to live with a more or less permanent sleep deficit, a factor that—by way of compensation—may help them to fall asleep after stressful weekdays. Both the insufficient sleep duration during the week and the long "recovery" nights on weekends could be accounted for in this manner.

Sleep Deprivation and the Stages of Sleep

It has already been pointed out that staying awake for days at a time does not mean that a person must then sleep for days to recover. Randy Gardner lost almost ninety hours of sleep when he set his world record, but after the experiment he slept for only seven hours longer than on a normal night. The question arises whether sleep in such cases, after a long period of waking, is somehow deeper or more intense. Does the distribution of the stages of sleep in EEG recordings provide any information about how this astonishing recovery process during the first period of sleep takes place?

In sleep deprivation experiments in which the first period of "recovery" sleep has been recorded in a laboratory, the results indicate that the main increase takes place in the percentage of deep sleep. After a waking period of some two hundred hours, for example, the percentage of deep sleep in the first nine hours of the recovery period rises to more than double its level in an ordinary night. Other experiments have also shown that long periods of waking cause particularly sensitive reactions in deep sleep; in these tests only a single sleepless night led to an increase. The conclusion may reasonably be drawn that this rise in the amount of deep sleep could represent an increase in sleep "intensity."

Things look quite different in the case of REM sleep. Its percentage may increase after a long period of sleep deprivation (up to 57 percent more during the first 9 hours of recovery sleep after 205 hours of waking time, for example); however, a short period of sleep deprivation (up to four days) does not show any increase in REM sleep during the first recovery night as a rule. A rise in REM sleep may occur, somewhat delayed, in a second recovery night.

Experiments in sleep deprivation suggest the existence of different regulatory mechanisms for deep sleep and REM sleep. While deep-sleep percentages rise immediately and after only brief sleep deprivation, REM sleep levels change only after a relatively long period of waking. Experiments that were aimed not at depriving the participants of sleep altogether but only at reducing the total sleeping time also confirm the high priority of deep sleep. In the test of the four couples described before, in which they gradually reduced the duration of their nightly sleep by between one and a half and three and a half hours, it emerged that the length of their deep-sleep stage 4 increased even though the total sleep period was shorter; on the other hand the amount of time spent in REM sleep dropped. The reduction of total sleep time occurred mainly at the expense of stage 2. Other experiments confirm that when the total amount of sleep is reduced, deep-sleep stages remain constant or grow even longer, while REM sleep stages become shorter.

We saw earlier (in chapter 2) that the division of non-REM sleep into different stages rests on rather arbitrary criteria and that the technique of EEG spectral analysis provides a far more accurate picture of the continuous changes taking place in the brain during sleep. Since deep sleep is characterized by a high percentage of slow waves in the delta frequency range (1–4 Hz), we investigated the effects of a short period of sleep deprivation on slow EEG waves. Figure 10.2 illustrates the results, which were recorded in experiments on human beings and rats. It is evident in both cases that sleep deprivation leads to a significant

Person Before Sleep Deprivation

After Sleep Deprivation

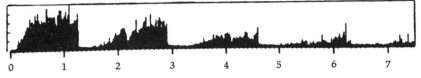

0   1   2   3   4   5   6   7

Rat Before Sleep Deprivation

After Sleep Deprivation

0   1   2   3   4   5

Time (in Hours)

FIGURE 10.2

Sleep Deprivation Increases the Percentage of Slow EEG Waves in Person and Rat.

The illustration shows spectral recordings of slow waves (1–4 Hz) in a sleep EEG. Man: after 40.5 hours without sleep (cf. figure 2.6). Rat: after 24 hours without sleep (cf. figure 7.7).

increase in slow EEG waves and that the periodic peaks, corresponding to phases of deep sleep, are higher and broader than in the control periods. Sleep deprivation is clearly reflected by the slow-wave activity of the sleep EEG. We shall return to this important finding in another context in the last chapter.

Selective Deprivation of Sleep Stages

Not long ago my colleagues and I performed an experiment at the sleep laboratory in Zurich in which we selectively deprived a subject of REM sleep for three consecutive nights. Robert, a medical student who had taken part in previous experiments, was willing to serve as a subject. He went to bed at his usual time, after the customary electrodes had been attached to his scalp, face, and chin. We monitored his sleep on the EEG polygraph record. After the first period of deep sleep, the recording announced the onset of REM sleep: the EEG curve flattened out, showing the typical small, rapid waves, and muscle tension disappeared. We immediately went into the next room and woke Robert up, asking him to mark on a scale whether he felt his sleep had been deep or light. We asked him a few further questions and then allowed him to go back to sleep. As is shown in figure 10.3, REM sleep began to set in with increasing frequency as the night went on. If we analyze the recordings of the three successive nights of the experiment, we can see that the

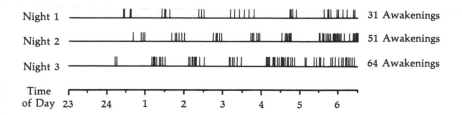

FIGURE 10.3
Awakenings to Ensure REM Sleep Deprivation
on Three Successive Nights.
The "REM sleep pressure" increases during deprivation of REM sleep. A test subject was awakened at the start of every REM sleep episode for three nights and so prevented from getting any REM sleep. The vertical lines indicate the awakenings. Their number increases from night to night. (From an experiment performed in collaboration with T. Niggli.)

number of times it was necessary to wake Robert up, in order to keep him from getting any REM sleep, rose from night to night. It is interesting to note that depriving him of this stage of sleep produced an increasing "pressure" for REM sleep but that this pressure was not continuous throughout the night. It appeared only periodically; between the periods in which we had to wake him frequently, Robert spent periods of about an hour in uninterrupted non-REM sleep. Toward the end of the third night, the onsets of REM sleep became so frequent that he returned to REM sleep only a few seconds after having been aroused, so we had to disturb his sleep at very short intervals.

REM-sleep-deprivation experiments were first performed by William Dement in the 1960s. At that time, only a few years after the discovery of REM sleep, the opinion prevailed in scientific circles that dreams occurred only in this stage, so REM sleep deprivation was equated with dream deprivation. It was an unfortunate coincidence that Dement thought he could observe an increased irritability and lack of concentration in the subjects of his very first experiment. This led to the conclusion that dreaming was indispensable for a healthy state of psychic equilibrium. Dement himself retracted this opinion after conducting more thorough tests, and subsequent experiments conducted by other research groups have confirmed that depriving people of REM sleep causes no psychic disturbances whatsoever. Nonetheless, the mistaken belief that REM sleep deprivation has particularly devastating effects has persisted to the present day.

If test subjects are deprived of REM sleep for several days in a row, an increase in the percentage of REM sleep may occur in the recovery nights. This makes it appear as if the organism were making up for a deficit of this stage. However, such a "REM sleep rebound" has not been observed in all cases and may even—as in our own experiment with Robert—fail to take place altogether. The hypothesis has been proposed that these individual differences are related to the personality of the test subject.

We have seen in this chapter that the effects of total sleep deprivation on slow EEG waves are very similar for human beings and rats. The same similarity of reactions applies to REM sleep, for a REM sleep rebound has been shown also to occur in various kinds of animals that have been subjected either to total sleep deprivation or to selective REM sleep deprivation. This finding indicates that not only the sleep stages but also their basic regulatory mechanisms are essentially the same in all mammals.

So far our discussion of selective sleep deprivation has concentrated on REM sleep. Is it possible to bring about deprivation of other stages? A selective deprivation of all non-REM sleep cannot be realized since the non-REM stage comprises 75–80 percent of total sleep and non-REM sleep deprivation would therefore be tantamount to complete deprivation. It is, however, possible to prevent test subjects from getting any deep sleep. In experiments first undertaken in the early sixties, the participants were disturbed at every initiation of stage 4. The stimuli were not strong enough to wake them up but did cause them to shift to a more superficial stage of non-REM sleep. In this manner the occurrence of deep sleep could be largely prevented, just as was done in the REM sleep deprivation experiments. It could be observed that in these tests the participants once again had to be disturbed repeatedly. A stage 4 rebound took place in the following period of recovery sleep. An interpretation of these findings is not easily arrived at, because deep sleep can be distinguished from the other non-REM stages only on the basis of its high percentage of slow EEG waves. A selective deprivation of deep sleep can cause an increase in slow EEG waves in other stages, however, a compensatory phenomenon that we have observed in our own experiments. For this reason a selective deprivation of deep sleep is more difficult to bring about than deprivation of REM sleep and can be only partially successful.

Sleep Deprivation as a Therapy for Depression

Endogenous depressions are, along with schizophrenia, among the most important forms of serious mental illness. Feelings of hopelessness, despair, and guilt typically prevail in such patients. In severe cases they are no longer willing or able to act on their own initiative, since everything appears to them equally meaningless and insurmountably difficult. For many such severely depressed people, taking their own lives seems the only way out of their torment.

Sleep disturbances are often an early symptom of depressive illness. The sleep of depressive patients is superficial, and they wake up often at night. Early-morning insomnia is a frequent form of depressive sleep disorder. It is therefore astonishing, but true, that total deprivation of this already disturbed sleep leads to a definite improvement in the condition of many depressed patients. This form of treatment has been under systematic investigation by a number of research teams ever since the favorable effect of sleep deprivation was first discovered in the late sixties.

How does sleep deprivation therapy proceed? The patient— or a group of patients—is kept awake during the night by the staff of the psychiatric hospital. Depending on the severity of their condition, the patients spend the night playing cards, reading, taking walks, or pursuing some manual activity. If they number among the fortunate 40 percent of the depressed patients who respond well to this treatment, their condition improves by the early morning hours. They become more communicative and active; their mood brightens. This phenomenon is particularly impressive when it occurs in cases where the depression has persisted for many weeks. The improvement in the patient's condition generally lasts into the following day and may even take a further rise. Unfortunately, the first sleep period that follows usually causes a relapse into depression, and only in very few cases has a prolonged improvement been observed. The all-too-brief success of this type of therapy obviously limits its practical usefulness, and the burden it places on the hospital staff is considerable.

At present, various research groups are investigating ways of modifying sleep-deprivation therapy to produce longer-lasting benefits and to reduce its cost in personnel and time. The first results indicate that long-term improvements of depression may be attainable through a combination of sleep deprivation and antidepressant medication. There have also been reports that a reduction of sleep by a few hours can have a beneficial effect. For scientists engaged in basic research the fact that a simple change in the sleep/wake cycle produces a definite antidepressant effect presents a fascinating but still unsolved riddle. The solution of this problem could bring us closer to the understanding of the biological basis of depression. In the last chapter we will discuss a hypothesis based on a model of sleep regulation that could contain the germ of an answer.

11

Sleep as a Biological Rhythm

Many people namely believe that it matters not at all when they sleep these seven hours, whether in the daytime or at night. They indulge in their studies or pleasures as late into the night as possible and believe that it is all the same if they sleep on into the morning the same number of hours that they robbed from midnight. But I must ask everyone who values his good health to beware of this seductive error.

—C. W. HUFELAND
Die Kunst, das menschliche Leben zu verlängern (1798)

Most people in our part of the world go to bed at about the same time and get up at the same time, year in and year out. Slight variations may occur on weekends, holidays, or vacations, but the regularity of our rest/activity rhythm is strikingly documented by long-term recordings. Figure 11.1 shows the rest/activity pattern of a professionally active man who wore a small recording device on his wrist for over a year. The rest phase lasted approximately six and a half to seven hours, usually from 12:30 to 7:30 A.M. The two obvious breaks in the rhythmic patterns were caused by trips from Europe to the United States and the resulting shift in time zones.

We are seldom in a position to choose freely the times at which we go to bed and get up; they are normally determined to a large degree by our family lives, schools, jobs, and other

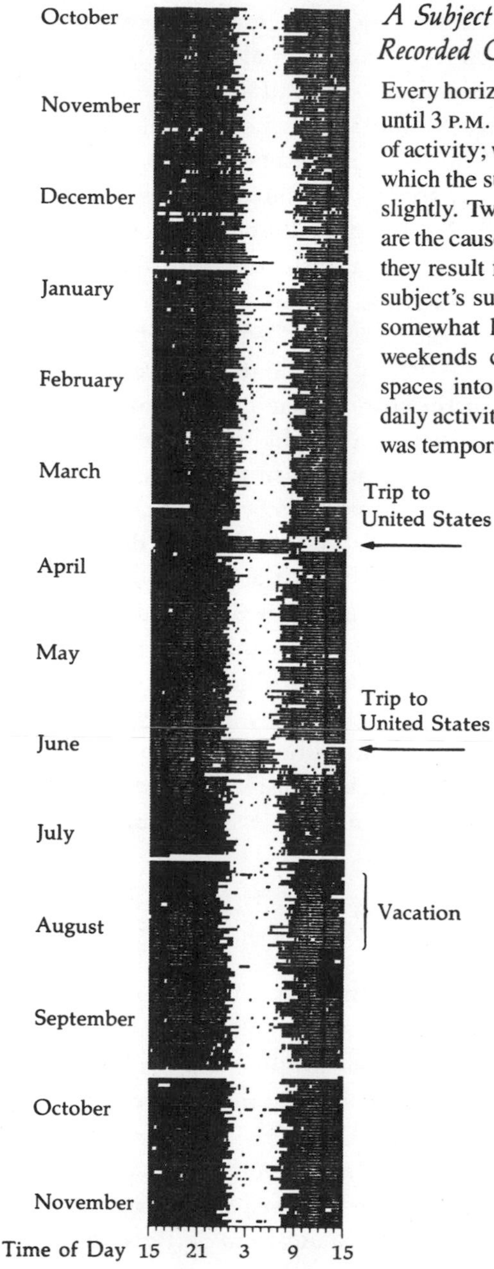

FIGURE 11.1

A Subject's Rest/Activity Rhythm that Was Recorded Continuously for More than a Year.

Every horizontal line represents one day (from 3 P.M. until 3 P.M. on the next day). Lines represent periods of activity; white spaces, periods of rest. The times at which the subject got up and went to bed varied only slightly. Two trips from Europe to the United States are the cause of the two obvious breaks in the pattern; they result from the shift in time zones. During the subject's summer vacation his total sleeping time is somewhat longer. The fact that he got up later on weekends causes the periodic extension of white spaces into the morning hours. In cases where no daily activity is registered at all, the recording device was temporarily out of order.

social and cultural factors. There are many reasons why we generally sleep at night. From time immemorial human beings have withdrawn into their dwellings at nightfall, since opportunities for active pursuits were limited by darkness, while risks and dangers were great. The hours after sunset were devoted to home and family, and spent preparing for the night's rest. The invention of artificial electric light, which illuminates not only single dwellings but entire cities, has transformed our lives by making it possible to carry daytime activities over into the evening hours. This example of "progress," which Webb has called the Edison effect, tempts many people to increase their leisure time in the evening at the cost of their sleep. Television carries entertainment into every household until the small hours, making people feel that they are missing something by going to bed. An early bedtime becomes an act of renunciation. It is often tempting to let external circumstances dictate whether we go to bed early or late. But is it actually possible to postpone or alter one's bedtime entirely at will, according to how one may happen to feel? What would happen if a person could go to bed and get up just as he liked, without any outside pressures or knowledge of what time of day it was? What would a "paradise" of unlimited opportunities for sleep be like? If such exceptional conditions existed, would sleeping and waking occur in random sequence, or would a certain rhythm still persist?

A "Time-free" Environment

Even if we lived alone, without clocks and in complete isolation, we would still not be able to escape the influence of day and night on our lives completely. Daylight, the sounds of nature, and the noises of our environment would keep us informed about the approximate time of day. Supposing we wanted to eliminate every external indication of time, we would either have to travel to the far north, where the sun shines almost twenty-four hours a day in summer, or else go deep underground, where neither light nor sounds could reach us.

In the early 1960s scientists began to investigate how people behave when for a period of days or even weeks they do not know what time it is. Those were the years in which mankind was preparing to explore the moon and the nearer regions of the universe. Space travel fascinated scientists and politicians alike, so enormous government grants became available for biomedical research. One major question was whether astronauts would be able to adapt to extraterrestrial conditions. The interest of aerospace administrations in these problems stimulated basic research on human biological rhythms, a field that had until then been largely neglected. Michel Siffre, a courageous young French explorer of caves, shifted his studies from geology to biology at that time. Along with his associates he spent weeks and months in total isolation far below the surface of the earth, in order to study the effects of such conditions on the human organism. In these experiments in cold, damp caves that were not always entirely safe, he ingeniously combined science and adventure.

Jürgen Aschoff, the director of the Max Planck Institute for Behavioral Physiology in Erling-Andechs (Bavaria), and one of his associates, the physicist Rütger Wever, approached the same research problems in a more sober and efficient spirit. They remodeled an empty bunker near Munich, turning it into an experimental research station where two people could each spend weeks in isolation. Each test participant could exist comfortably in his own area, which contained a main room, a kitchen, a toilet, and a shower. The rooms in the bunker were constructed to screen out all outside noise and light but were provided with a dumbwaiter through which the subject could make contact with the external world. Of course, during the experiments no clocks, radios, or other devices were allowed that could have provided a time clue. As the tests proceeded, various data were measured. Motor activity was recorded by sensors in the floor, and body temperature by a rectal probe. In some of the experiments, psychological tests were administered periodically and the chemical composition of the subjects' urine was analyzed. Wever compiled the results of his observation of more than two hundred test participants in his recently published book *The Circadian System of Man.*

Before we turn to the results of these experiments, let us consider an obvious question: How do the participants feel during these solitary weeks, and how do they pass the time? According to the reports of Wever and his colleagues, the great majority of the subjects regarded their experiences as very positive, and many of them were eager to participate in further experiments. What makes such a period of isolation so pleasant? Is it perhaps the freedom from all responsibility and commitments for a few weeks, the opportunity to do exactly as one pleases? Or does the cause lie deeper, namely, in experiencing how biological rhythms can run their natural course without interference? The answer must remain open for the time being.

Most test subjects spend their time reading, writing, and listening to music; college students sometimes make use of the opportunity to study for exams in peace and quiet. It happened again and again that participants were surprised to be told that the time was up. An experiment in a cave, conducted by Siffre and his colleagues, also demonstrated the typical underestimation of the elapsed time: when the experiment's period of five months was over, the subject was convinced that he had spent only three months in isolation. The changes in sleep/wake patterns that occur in isolation will soon show us how such a misjudgment may arise.

Figure 11.2 is a diagram of the sleep/wake cycle of a person who for the first three days of the experiment is aware of the time of day; he habitually sleeps from 11 P.M. to 7 A.M. From the fourth day on, all time information is withheld. Our test subject goes to bed forty minutes later than usual on this first day without a clock and does not get up until eight o'clock on the

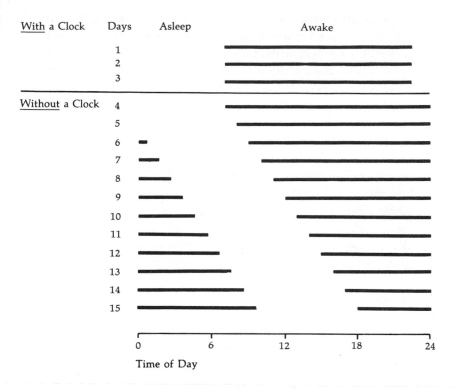

FIGURE 11.2
Schematic Representation of an Isolation Experiment in a Bunker.
(An "Internal Clock" Times the Sleep/Wake Rhythm.)
During the first three days the subject sleeps from 11 P.M. to 7 A.M. During
the next twelve days, without a clock, he goes to bed every day one hour
later than on the preceding day. The human "internal clock" runs with
a periodicity of about twenty-five hours.

following morning. He is not aware of this change, however.
On each succeeding day he goes to bed and gets up one hour
later than on the day before. The participant's "subjective" day
thus contains not the usual twenty-four hours but twenty-five
instead. On the thirteenth day without time information (the
sixteenth day of the experiment), he goes to bed at 10:40 A.M.
instead of 11 P.M. and gets up at eight o'clock in the evening.

The phase of his sleep/wake cycle has now shifted by exactly twelve hours. If the experiment were to continue, we would find that after twenty-five days the participant would have experienced only twenty-four "subjective" days. Living in an environment containing no external time indicators, he would by his own reckoning have grown only twenty-four days older, rather than twenty-five, and would have gained one day!

If the experiment were extended over a period of several weeks, the subject's wake period might suddenly increase from seventeen hours to almost thirty-four hours and his sleeping time from just over eight hours to almost seventeen! In other words: the subject would change over from a twenty-five-hour day to a fifty-hour day, but he would once again not be aware of this drastic alteration in his sleep/wake rhythm. By the end of the experiment the number of days he would have subjectively experienced would lie far below the number of days that had actually passed.

Whether the participant's subjective day contains twenty-five or fifty hours, the sleep/wake ratio usually changes little. In our example the subject spends about one-third of his time asleep in the temporal-isolation schedule, just as he does under normal conditions. For a short sleeper the sleep/wake ratio would also remain small in a "time-free" environment, even though the length of time he spent asleep would increase in absolute terms.

Under these conditions the distribution of sleep stages shows some typical changes: although REM sleep episodes normally increase in length from cycle to cycle (see chapter 2), this is no longer true in the bunker. The first REM sleep episode occurs here soon after the subject falls asleep—that is, REM sleep latency is brief, and the length of the first episode is similar to those that follow. The percentage of REM sleep remains unchanged. But, in contrast to REM sleep, the distribution of deep sleep is changed little by temporal isolation.

As has already been mentioned, the record in figure 11.2 shows a sleep/wake rhythm of twenty-five hours. This period length was chosen for the illustration because it corresponds to the average period of the body temperature rhythm, which Wever found to be close to twenty-five hours. It can vary in individuals; one person may have a rhythm of 24.7 hours, another 25.2, but more important than the exact length of these periods is the fact that every person maintains his own rhythm over an extended time to an amazingly accurate degree. The biological rhythms that we observe in this situation obviously differ from the twenty-four-hour periodicity of the earth's rotation, and so it appears unlikely that they are caused by a hidden environmental influence. They must be generated by an "internal clock" within the organism.

Where Is Our Internal Clock Located?

The heliotrope reacts to sunlight and the day: its leaves and stems contract and close toward sunset. The same reaction may be seen if one touches the plant or shakes it. Monsieur de Mairan has established that sunlight and air are not necessary for this phenomenon to take place and that the reaction is only slightly less pronounced if the plant is kept in complete darkness. It continues to open very distinctly at sunrise, closes again in the evening, and remains closed the whole night. The heliotrope plant thus responds to the sun without being exposed to it in any way. . . . Monsieur de Mairan invites botanists and physicians to pursue this observation even though they, too, might prefer to devote their time to other problems. The true study of physics, which can only consist of experimental physics, necessarily shows only very slow progress.[1]

This passage on his observations of the heliotrope was published by Jean Jacques Dortous de Mairan in the proceedings of the Royal Academy of Sciences in Paris in the year 1729. The

HISTOIRE·
DE
L'ACADEMIE
ROYALE
DES SCIENCES.

ANNÉE M. DCCXXJX.

Avec les Mémoires de Mathématique & de Physique,
pour la même Année.

Tirés des Regiſtres de cette Académie.

A PARIS,
DE L'IMPRIMERIE ROYALE
M. DCCXXXI.

FIGURE 11.3

*Title Page of the Proceedings of the Royal Academy of Sciences
in Paris from the Year 1729 (Paris: Imprimerie Royale, 1731).*
In this volume de Mairan presented the first description of diurnal
plant rhythms.

twenty-four-hour rhythm in the movement of plant leaves—
which, he saw, persisted even in darkness—was the first indication that biological rhythms may occur in the absence of environmental influences. This report published more than 250
years ago was correct not only regarding the observation of the
heliotrope, but also in its predictions about the slow progress
of science: De Mairan's discovery was not systematically investigated by other scientists until the present century.

One of the first modern scientists to study plant rhythms was Erwin Bünning, a professor of botany at the University of Tübingen, in Germany. Subsequently, scientific interest shifted progressively from plants to animals. Pioneering experiments in rhythm research were performed by the two "fathers" of chronobiology (the study of biological rhythms)—the British biologist Colin Pittendrigh, who works in the United States, and the German behavioral physiologist Jürgen Aschoff. At the first major conference on chronobiology, at Cold Spring Harbor, New York, in 1960, it became evident that twenty-four-hour rhythms are pervasive in nature. As we have already seen from the experiments in man, the rhythms of animals also usually correspond to the day/night cycle of their environment, but they persist even when external influences are removed. Here, too, "internal clocks" must be responsible for maintaining biorhythmical processes.

When organisms live in temporal isolation, the periodicity of their daily rhythms normally deviates from twenty-four hours. Franz Halberg, a chronobiologist working in the United States, coined the term *circadian rhythms,* which is in standard use today (from the Latin words *circa,* "about," and *dies,* "day"). In the absence of time information, a "free-running" circadian rhythm manifests itself. A great deal of intensive research work has been devoted to circadian rhythms in the last twenty years: zoologists have studied their development in insects, mollusks, and other invertebrates, while cell biologists have searched for their origins in one-celled organisms. The central question concerns the physiological structures and biological processes responsible for circadian rhythms.

Let us look at a concrete example. An experiment was conducted on the motor activity of rats, which was measured by a device attached to the bottom of their cages. In figure 11.4 periods of activity (above a certain threshold) are depicted as black bars; the white spaces represent periods of rest. The measurements for two successive days have been placed next to one another in order to make the changes more clearly visible. The

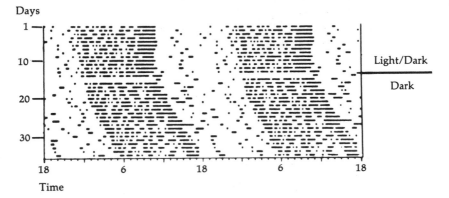

FIGURE 11.4

An "Internal Clock" Governs the Rest/Activity
Rhythm of a Rat Living in Permanent Darkness.

Horizontal bars represent periods of activity; white spaces, periods of rest. In order to illustrate the rhythmic displacements clearly, two days are shown next to each other on each line (i.e., days 1 and 2 on the top line, days 2 and 3 on the next line, and so on). In the first two weeks the animal lives under normal conditions: twelve hours of light, twelve hours of darkness. In the following three weeks complete darkness is maintained. The rest/activity rhythm persists, but the end of the active period is delayed on each succeeding day by about twenty-five minutes. The circadian rhythm generated by the "internal clock" is thus longer than twenty-four hours.

top line records the rest/activity behavior of the rat for days 1 and 2 of the experiment, the second line for days 2 and 3, and so on. For the first fourteen days the animal was kept under artificial conditions of light and darkness, the period of light lasting from 11 A.M. to 11 P.M. It is obvious how much the rest/activity rhythm is influenced by the light conditions. The rat is a nocturnal animal, active during darkness and resting during periods of light. From day 15 on, this experiment consisted of maintaining the rat in complete darkness around the clock. It was kept in a soundproof chamber without any light and received no information whatever about the time of day. As we have already seen with regard to human beings, rest/activity rhythms by no means disappear under such conditions. Their periodicity does change, however, and no longer consists of twenty-four hours. In this experiment the periodicity of the rat's behavior also lengthened. As the illustration shows, the periods of rest and activity were gradually delayed each day in comparison with the control period at the beginning.

We can see from this experiment that the light/dark cycle of the environment represents a very important source of time information for the circadian rhythms of rats; this is true of most other animals as well. In the technical language of chronobiology, light is termed a zeitgeber, that is, an external signal that synchronizes the circadian rhythms of an organism (see chapter 7). Such synchronization does not require that the period of light last twelve hours. Numerous experiments have shown that much shorter exposures to light (usually fifteen to sixty minutes, but in extreme cases one flash of light) are sufficient to synchronize the phase of circadian rhythms.

We have so far been considering the relation of circadian rhythms to the environment, and now it is time to turn to the question of their origin. In the 1920s, Curt Richter, a professor at Johns Hopkins University, began extensive experiments on the rest/activity rhythms of rats, and observed that circadian rhythms are hardly influenced by various manipulations. He kept his laboratory animals at different temperatures, exposed them to hunger, thirst, and stress, removed hormone glands, destroyed regions of their brains, and gave them various drugs. None of these measures had any effect on the periodicity or the phase of the circadian rest/activity rhythm. Richter did not observe any changes until he removed large sections of the rats' interbrain, an observation that led him to speculate that the "internal clock" must be located in this part of the brain. His idea proved to be right.

In 1972 two experimental psychologists from the University

of California at Berkeley, Fred Stephan and Irving Zucker, published a paper that represented a major breakthrough for the whole field of biological rhythms. They reported that in rats the elimination of a small, circumscribed area of the interbrain caused the circadian rhythms of rest/activity and water intake to disappear completely. After this surgical intervention, the animals' motor activity and drinking behavior became randomly distributed throughout the day. They were able, however, to maintain their intake of liquid at normal levels and showed no major differences in their behavior. The crucial anatomical structure proved to be a nucleus of the interbrain, one by two millimeters in size, which lies deep in the brain, directly above the crossing of the optical nerves (called the chiasma opticum). Figure 11.5 illustrates the effect of removing these "suprachiasmatic nuclei" on the rest/activity rhythm of rats. Compared with that of normal animals, their rhythm has disappeared entirely, and their bouts of activity occur in irregular sequences spread out over a twenty-four-hour day. In collaboration with Irene Tobler and Gerard Groos, we have investigated whether the disappearance of the circadian sleep/wake rhythm may also disrupt the regulation of deep sleep and REM sleep. We found that arrhythmic animals also react to sleep deprivation with an increase in deep sleep and REM sleep, and concluded that the circadian sleep/wake rhythm, on the one hand, and sleep regulation as a function of prior waking, on the other, are controlled by separate mechanisms.

The discovery by Stephan and Zucker was followed by numerous further experiments confirming that the destruction of suprachiasmatic nuclei causes circadian rhythms to disappear. The next question to arise was whether these areas really represent the long-sought location of the "internal clock," or whether they are merely important coordination centers of the system that governs rhythms. To try to find an answer, two researchers at the renowned Mitsubishi Institute near Tokyo, Shin-ichi Inouye and Hiroshi Kawamura, performed experi-

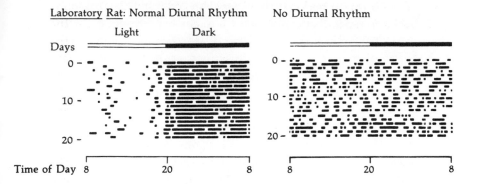

FIGURE 11.5
Circadian Rhythms Disappear When Certain
Nerve Cells in the Interbrain Are Destroyed.
Left-hand diagram: normal twenty-four-hour rhythm of a rat. The animal
is active mainly at night (in darkness). Right-hand diagram: after elimination of the suprachiasmatic nerve cells in the interbrain, the rhythm disappears completely. Rest and activity are randomly distributed throughout
the day.

ments with rats whose nerve fiber connections between the
suprachiasmatic nuclei of the interbrain and the rest of the
brain had been severed. Tiny implanted electrodes recorded the
nerve cell activity of the region isolated by this means, while
other electrodes recorded activity in other areas of the brain. As
expected, after the fibers had been severed, all signs of circadian
rhythms disappeared both from the animals' behavior and from
the electrical activity of the brain regions outside the interbrain.
The isolated suprachiasmatic nuclei, on the other hand, continued to exhibit a circadian rhythm in the discharge pattern of
their nerve cells. Obviously, a circadian rhythm persists in this
area even when it is not connected to other parts of the brain.

There is strong evidence, therefore, that circadian rhythms
may originate in the suprachiasmatic nuclei themselves. Nevertheless, several questions remain unanswered, and the discus-

sion continues as to whether other structures outside this region can also generate rhythms, or may at least become a "substitute" clock if the "main" clock is damaged.

Free-Running Rhythms

In the late fifties a British scientist named Mary Lobban and her colleagues conducted an unusual experiment. They spent a summer with some experimental subjects in the far north of Norway, in Spitsbergen, where the polar day gives no cues about the time of day. The twelve participants were divided into two groups and given wristwatches to wear that had been manipulated without their knowledge. For one of the groups the watches' mechanisms had been speeded up, so that the hour hand completed a full revolution in only ten and a half hours instead of the normal twelve. The other group wore watches that had been slowed down, so that the hour hand took thirteen and a half hours to go around once in their case. The sleep/wake rhythm of the participants adapted itself immediately to these changed conditions; they adopted a twenty-one-hour or twenty-seven-hour day without realizing it. Not all the biological rhythms of their bodies could be fooled by the manipulated watches, however. The concentration of potassium in their urine continued to vary with a rhythm of almost exactly twenty-four hours, for example. The subjects were experiencing what is called internal desynchronization, a phenomenon that occurs when some of the body's biological rhythms are out of phase with others, so that their sensitively attuned rhythmical system becomes disordered.

A desynchronization of the sleep/wake rhythm in relation to other circadian rhythms has often been observed in isolation experiments. Body temperature usually exhibited a stable rhythm with a periodicity of twenty-five hours, even if the periods of the sleep/wake rhythm varied to a much greater degree. The differing length of these periods led to constantly changing phase relationships between the various rhythms. When experiments are conducted in a "time-free" environment, they begin with all the subject's rhythms in a state of synchronization, with sleep onset normally coinciding with the low point of the temperature cycle. As internal desynchronization arises, the subject goes to bed every day during a different phase of his temperature cycle. The temperature rhythm clearly exerts some influence on sleep, however, in spite of the shifting phase relationship. Jürgen Zulley, a chronobiologist in Erling-Andechs, has observed that a period of sleep beginning at the lowest point of the temperature cycle is usually shorter than one beginning when the cycle is at its peak. Correspondingly, times when subjects fell asleep tended to cluster around the falling arm of the temperature curve, whereas waking times were concentrated on the rising arm.

Does the brain contain one, two, or even more "internal clocks," which govern the rhythms of different processes in the human body? (They are referred to as "circadian oscillators" in the technical terminology of chronobiology.) The American research team of the late Elliot Weitzman (Montefiore Hospital, New York) and Richard Kronauer (Harvard University) has postulated the existence of two oscillators: a stable one with a periodicity of almost twenty-five hours, which is responsible for the rhythms of temperature, the adrenal hormone cortisol, and REM sleep; and a second, labile oscillator governing the sleep/wake rhythm. Serge Daan and Domien Beersma of the University of Groningen (Holland) and I have reached a different conclusion: namely, that one oscillator is sufficient to explain the available experimental data. According to our hypothesis, internal desynchronization of the sleep/wake rhythm in relation to other rhythms can be explained by assuming that two processes underlie sleep regulation: a "relaxation process" that exhibits an upswing during waking hours and a downswing during sleep, and a circadian process. The model on which this hypothesis is based will be discussed in greater detail in the final chapter.

Disturbances of Biological Rhythms as an Occupational Hazard

The sailors who circumnavigated the globe in earlier times often had to contend with difficult conditions, but they had one advantage over modern globe-trotters: they did not suffer from jet lag, that unpleasant consequence of air travel that more and more people know about from their own experience. After a long flight from east to west, the traveler wakes up in the new surroundings at an unusually early hour for several days, but feels dead tired in the middle of the afternoon. Travelers in an easterly direction usually find it hard to fall asleep at night. The main cause of these problems lies in the fact that our circadian rhythms take a while to adjust to a change in the day/night cycle. If a person flies from Europe to the United States, his metabolic and hormonal rhythms are still running on European time. Detailed studies have shown that it can take up to two weeks for rhythms to adapt completely to a major change of time zones. Many people find it much more pleasant to travel from east to west than vice versa; this could be because free-running circadian rhythms have, on the average, a periodicity of twenty-five hours: the temporary lengthening of the normal twenty-four-hour rhythm, which travel in a westerly direction requires, is easier for the body to accomplish than a shortening of rhythms to a cycle of less than twenty-four hours.

Although travelers may experience such rhythm displacements as unpleasant, they are fortunately only a temporary source of discomfort. People whose jobs require them to shift their rhythms frequently face a much more serious problem. The crews who work on long-distance flights are one such group, but the largest one consists of people employed in jobs on shifts outside normal office hours. In most industrialized countries they constitute approximately 20 percent of the total work force. Workers who have to change shifts often, and who must repeatedly adjust their circadian rhythms to new circumstances, may experience considerable difficulties.

It is hardly surprising that many people in such jobs suffer from sleep problems. Their main complaints are trouble in falling asleep, frequent awakenings in the night, and generally too little sleep. Noise levels in the environment, which are naturally higher during the day than at night, may add to their troubles. As a result, workers on night shifts get two to three hours less sleep during the daytime than when they can work on a day shift and sleep at night. In addition to their rhythm disturbances, they can accumulate a sleep deficit that impairs even further their general well-being and ability to function. Many such people turn to pills as the only way they see of getting a few good hours' sleep. A poll taken recently among airline flight crews indicated that their consumption of sleeping pills was much higher on working days than on free days.

Many health problems can be traced to the "rigidity" of circadian processes. When working hours change suddenly and remain at the new time for an extended period, the body's metabolic and hormonal rhythms need time to adjust, although the sleep/wake cycle must usually be changed immediately. A person in such a situation must then sleep at a time that his "internal clock" has programmed for being awake: his temperature, the blood level of the stress hormone adrenalin, and his kidney function are at high levels, while the secretion of melatonin (the hormone of the pineal gland) is minimal. In the first phase of such a shift, people often sleep poorly; they wake up frequently and feel unrefreshed. Analogous problems occur in their waking hours, since their circadian rhythms are programmed for rest. The consequences are often fatigue, lack of concentration, and a drop in performance levels.

Some people have extremely strong reactions to changes in

their daily rhythms and are practically incapable of performing demanding tasks at unaccustomed times of day. Other people can adapt more easily to such new situations. It is not clear how these individual differences arise; at present scientists know only that adaptation to rhythm displacement grows more difficult with advancing age.

It would be a mistake, however, to assume that the manifold problems of shift work arise solely from desynchronized circadian rhythms. The changes in working hours can also affect family relationships and make it difficult to lead a normal social life. Shift workers can easily slip into a "time ghetto," a form of isolation caused by their unusual mealtimes and bedtimes.

Phase-shifting Rhythms as a Therapy

A few years ago the American neurologist and sleep researcher Elliot Weitzman, his co-worker Charles Czeisler, and their associates reported an unusual case of a sleep disorder. A young man had been suffering for a long time from an inability to fall asleep before two o'clock in the morning. Since his professional obligations forced him to get up at 7 A.M., he was always short of sleep during the week. He made up for this by sleeping until noon on the weekends. All attempts to treat this problem, from medication to psychotherapy, had been unsuccessful. It occurred to Weitzman and Czeisler that this was perhaps a case in which a rhythm disorder was making it impossible for the patient to shorten his circadian sleep/wake rhythm to less than twenty-four hours, so that he was not able to advance his bedtime to an earlier hour.

As we have already seen, adjusting to a time-zone displacement from east to west, which requires a lengthening of circadian rhythms, is generally easier than adjustment in the opposite direction. Bearing this in mind, Weitzman and Czeisler advised their patient to go to bed not earlier than usual but later. Their treatment thus consisted of an intentional lengthening of his sleep/wake rhythm, with the goal of moving his bedtime around the clock to the desired phase.

In practical terms this was achieved by having the young man go to bed every day three hours later than on the preceding day. After a few days of this treatment he was sleeping during the day and waking up in the early evening. (Of course, he had to take this time off from his job.) When a week had passed he had reached his goal: he went to bed at the ideal hour for him, 11 P.M., and had gotten the necessary amount of sleep by 7 A.M. The patient was cured, but he had to maintain an extremely regular bedtime to avoid slipping back into the situation before this treatment.

Since this first case Weitzman and his associates, as well as other researchers, have described and successfully treated a whole series of similar problems. This disorder has been given the name "delayed sleep phase syndrome."

Let us look at another instance of rhythm disorder in the field of medicine. In 1979 Tom Wehr, Anna Wirz-Justice, and other researchers at the National Institute of Mental Health in the United States published a report on their successful treatment of a woman suffering from a severe endogenous depression. She, too, had been previously treated with various forms of therapy, to no avail. The research team then tried to help this patient by advancing her bedtime by six hours. In other words, she went to bed at 5 P.M. instead of at 11 P.M. The theoretical considerations that prompted this treatment were as follows: Wehr and his colleagues had observed that the circadian rhythms of other depressive patients exhibited an abnormal phase relationship to their sleep/wake cycle. The onset of their sleep, for example, coincided with their daily temperature minimum and not—as in healthy people—with the falling phase of the temperature cycle. One could say that the sleep of these depressive patients was "internally delayed."

The researchers' question was whether such an abnormal phase relationship could be contributing to or causing the depressive illness of their patient. If this were true, normalization of the phase relationship should lead to an improvement in her condition. Moving her bedtime forward did in fact have the antidepressive effect they had hoped for. The improvement lasted for about two weeks, but by the end of that time her temperature rhythm had adapted completely to the new sleep/ wake rhythm, and the original phase imbalance recurred. Her depressive symptoms increased again at this point. When her bedtime was phase-advanced for a second time, these symptoms again disappeared for a time. The treatment of other patients was only partially successful, however, and further studies will be necessary before we can say whether this kind of rhythm therapy is of general usefulness in the treatment of depression.

Weitzman's and Wehr's reports on the treatment of their two patients, one with a sleep disorder and the other with depression, have one thing in common: the therapy in both cases consisted of a change in the patient's bedtime and in the period of the day spent asleep. This is a new and original approach to the treatment of diseases that used to be handled primarily with medication. Although these methods are still in the process of development and thus of more interest to research scientists than to the general practitioner, interesting new avenues of nondrug treatment are nonetheless beginning to open up. It has been known for some time that rhythm disturbances in the environment can seriously affect our well-being. What is new is the recognition that certain problems and illnesses may be caused by rhythm disturbances hidden within the human body itself. It may soon become possible to cure them with the appropriate form of rhythm therapy.

12

The Purpose of Sleep

The new mass of knowledge is still formless, incomplete,
lacking the essential threads of connection, displaying mis-
leading signals at every turn, riddled with blind alleys.
There are fascinating ideas all over the place, irresistible
experiments beyond numbering, all sorts of new ways into
the maze of problems. But every next move is unpredict-
able, every outcome uncertain. It is a puzzling time, but a
very good time.
                                                    —Lewis Thomas
              The Lives of a Cell: Notes of a Biology Watcher (1974)

As everyone knows, the need to sleep grows stronger the longer
we stay awake. A person who has not slept for a long time only
needs to sit down and he will nod off immediately. After the
onset of sleep, the "sleep pressure" diminishes progressively.
Sleep is deep at the beginning, but becomes more superficial as
the hours pass. This same phenomenon is reflected in the fact
that sleeping people shift position more frequently the longer
they have been asleep. We have already seen that the preva-
lence of slow EEG waves that characterize the deep-sleep stage
(stages 3 and 4) are a good indicator of the depth of non-REM
sleep. Slow waves are particularly in evidence in the first non-
REM/REM sleep cycle; then they taper off from cycle to cycle.
Their percentage is significantly increased after a person has
been sleep deprived (see chapter 10). This EEG parameter thus
appears to indicate a degree of sleep propensity, which is determined by the preceding amount of time spent awake. If some-

one lies down for a nap in the morning after a good night's sleep, he experiences less deep sleep than if he waited until the afternoon to go back to bed. In the same way a nap during the day reduces the amount of deep sleep the following night.

How are we to understand this need for sleep, which builds up as the day goes on? And how should we understand the increasing propensity for deep sleep that accompanies it? Is the kind of physical activity performed during the day one important factor? This question has been studied in different experiments. In one of them, marathon runners were used as subjects in order to investigate the effects of great physical exertion on sleep. Taken as a whole, the results of such studies are somewhat contradictory, however. In some studies a correlation was observed between physical activity and the deep sleep that followed, but in the majority of cases there was none.

Together with Mehmet Hanagasioglu I have addressed this problem in an animal experiment. We implanted permanent EEG and EMG electrodes in rats in order to obtain recordings of their brain waves and neck muscle tension by means of a miniature radio transmitter. The rats could move freely in their cage and also had access to a running wheel. In the active period of their sleep/wake rhythm, they logged up to seven kilometers (almost four and a half miles) on the wheel. When we then denied the rats access to the running wheel for two days, their opportunities for activity were sharply reduced. This drastic curtailment in locomotor activity induced virtually no change in the percentage of their deep sleep. Depriving them of sleep for twelve to twenty-four hours, on the other hand, produced a massive increase in both deep sleep and slow EEG waves (chapter 10). These findings indicate that a rise in sleep propensity is caused primarily by the length of the preceding waking time and not by a particular form of activity during this period.

Do We Fall Asleep Because It Is Time?

Experiments in which subjects were deprived of sleep have repeatedly shown that they had the greatest difficulty staying awake in the small hours of the morning. Their urge to sleep was all but irresistible at this point. Once they had managed to get through this critical period, it was not as hard to remain awake.

Figure 12.1 reproduces the results of an experiment conducted by the Swedish researchers Torbjörn Åkerstedt and Jan Fröberg, in which fifteen subjects had to stay awake for three days. Every three hours the participants were asked to assess

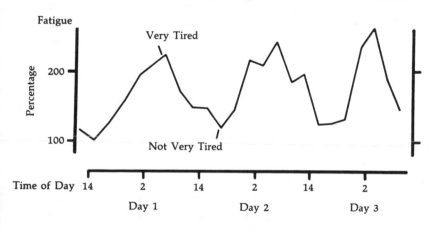

FIGURE 12.1
*Circadian Rhythm of Fatigue During Seventy-two Hours
of Sleep Deprivation.*

Test subjects spent seventy-two hours without sleep and rated their fatigue every three hours on a scale in comparison with their normal fatigue (= 100 percent). The feeling of fatigue was always highest in the early hours of the morning and lowest in the afternoon. The curve represents an average taken from fifteen subjects.

SOURCE: Adapted from T. Åkerstedt and J. E. Fröberg, "Psychophysiological Circadian Rhythms in Women During 72 Hours of Sleep Deprivation," *Waking and Sleeping* I (1977):387–94.

the degree of their fatigue and mark it on a scale, which expressed fatigue during the experiment in relation to normal fatigue (=100 percent). The curve of the average obtained shows obvious diurnal oscillations. Fatigue was lowest in the afternoon and reached a maximum in the early hours of the morning. Other, similar experiments, in which the degree of the subjects' fatigue rose even more clearly over the course of three days, also produced definite evidence of diurnal oscillations.

It is an interesting phenomenon that the rhythm of sleep propensity runs directly counter to the rhythm of body temperature. Sleep propensity is high when temperature has reached its daily minimum; it is low when temperature reaches its maximum. Such observations make it clear, as was mentioned in chapter 11, that sleep propensity is not determined solely by the length of time spent awake but is also strongly affected by a circadian process that is independent of sleeping and waking. On the face of our "internal clock," the time for sleep has been obviously engraved by nature.

Two Sleep Processes: A Model of Sleep Regulation

Both the amount of time we have previously spent awake and a circadian process are responsible for regulating our sleep. Figure 12.2 presents a model showing how these two factors operate in conjunction with one another. "Process S" indicates the level of sleep propensity during the daytime and the "depth" of sleep at night. This curve therefore rises during waking hours (as sleep propensity increases) and falls during sleep (as the percentage of deep sleep decreases). "Process C" corresponds to the circadian rhythm of sleep propensity, which is independent of prior sleep or waking. It is highest at 4 A.M., when it is particularly difficult to stay awake, and lowest at 4 P.M. The curve $\bar{C}$ depicted in the illustration represents not process C itself but its mirror image. Curve $\bar{C}$ can be considered

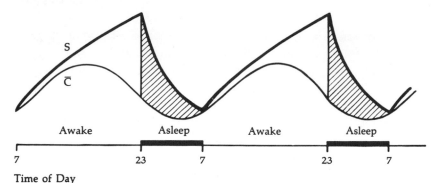

Sleep/Wake Cycle

S

C̄

Awake   Asleep   Awake   Asleep

7   23   7   23   7

Time of Day

Sleep Deprivation

S

C̄

Awake   Asleep

7   23   7   23   8

Time of Day

FIGURE 12.2

A Model of Sleep Regulation.

It is assumed that sleep occurs as a result of the combined action of process S and process C. The curve S is dependent upon sleep/wake behavior and declines during sleep. Process C is a circadian process governed by the circadian rhythm of the "internal clock"; it runs independently of sleeping and waking. The negative function of C is represented by the curve C̄ and can be considered a wake-up threshold that is modulated by a circadian rhythm. "Sleep pressure" is measured by the interval between the curves S and C̄. During sleep deprivation, S continues to rise. The period of recovery sleep that follows is more intensive but only slightly longer than normal. To simplify matters slightly, we can think of process S as an hourglass that is turned over every day when we fall asleep or wake up. But the oscillations of process C are independent of the actual time we spend asleep or awake and can be compared to the unvarying revolutions of a clock's hands.

as representing a wake threshold, so its lowest point corresponds to a maximum of sleep propensity. In this model we assume that process C can be influenced not only by our "internal clock" but also by external stimuli. A boring lecture, for example, can increase our sleepiness, whereas watching an exciting film can lead us to postpone our bedtime. The two-process model postulates that the effective sleep propensity is represented by the sum of processes S and C. This corresponds to the difference (or interval) between the curves S and C̄. Looking at the illustration, we can follow the paths of these curves and the intervals between them as the day progresses. After our subject wakes up at 7 A.M., the curves lie close together throughout the morning; this means that the desire to sleep is small. As the afternoon passes, the interval becomes progressively larger, until it reaches a maximum at bedtime (11 P.M.). During the course of the night, as we sleep, the interval between the two curves decreases progressively, until it reaches zero at the moment of waking (7 A.M.).

The lower part of the illustration indicates what happens if a person does not sleep for one whole night and the following day. Since sleep does not set in at 11 P.M., as it normally would, process S continues to rise. The interval between S and C̄ reaches a first maximum at four o'clock in the morning, the time of the "crisis." As more hours pass, the curves approach each other again, indicating a lessening of the urge to sleep. By the time the subject falls asleep the next evening at 11 P.M., S has reached a high value.

The large interval between the two curves corresponds to the deep non-REM sleep during the first part of the night, when slow EEG waves predominate. Since process S declines not as a diagonal line but rather as an exponential curve, the length of sleep after sleep deprivation is only slightly longer than normal. This model can also account for the results of experiments which showed that subjects were able to sleep only for a short time in the morning in spite of having spent the preceding night awake.

While the percentage of deep sleep depends mainly on the amount of prior waking time, REM sleep is largely determined by the circadian rhythm. We have accordingly assumed in our model that REM-sleep propensity is reflected by process C. In a more detailed version of this model—which cannot be presented here—we assumed that REM sleep and non-REM sleep show a mutual inhibitory action. Such an interaction may account for the cyclical recurrence of non-REM and REM sleep. Serge Daan and Domien Beersma of the University of Groningen have developed a computer model of sleep regulation based on similar assumptions and shown that it is possible to simulate the typical changes in the sleep/wake rhythm that occur in a "time-free" environment. Some of these changes, such as internal desynchronization and a periodicity of fifty hours, were described in chapter 11.

Of course, the model presented here is intended only as a working hypothesis; it certainly does not do full justice to the complexity of the sleep-regulating mechanisms. These ideas will probably require adaptations and modifications. Nevertheless, the modeling approach is useful for two reasons: first, the model enables us to integrate a considerable amount of experimental data within a single, conceptual framework; second, it allows us to make specific predictions, which can be tested by further experiments. Certain indications already exist about possible biological mechanisms that might underlie both processes described here. The rise in process S during waking and its drop during sleep, for instance, might very well correspond to oscillations in the level of an endogenous sleep substance, as was presumed to exist in the hypotheses of Piéron and his followers (chapter 9). Process C seems to reflect the operation of an "internal clock," which could be located in the suprachiasmatic nuclei of the interbrain (chapter 11) and which may regulate various rhythmic processes (such as temperature and cortisol levels) in addition to sleep. It is important to emphasize that the present model—unlike some other models—requires the existence of only a single oscillator.

Sleep Regulation and Depression

We have already pointed out elsewhere that people suffering from endogenous depressions generally do not sleep well, but that—paradoxically—their condition can be improved by a deprivation of sleep. The model of sleep regulation just described may provide some clues about the mechanisms relating sleep and depressive illness. In a collaborative project with Anna Wirz-Justice (a neurochemist and chronobiologist at the University of Basel, Switzerland), we have assumed that the sleep/wake–dependent process S may be impaired in patients suffering from endogenous depressions. As a consequence, the process would not rise to normal levels in the course of the waking hours (see figure 12.3). The resulting reduction in the interval between curves S and $\bar{C}$ leads to a lower sleep propensity. The assumption of an impaired process S could thus serve to explain the difficulty that depressive patients typically have in falling asleep as well as their frequent awakenings during the night. In addition, the figure shows that the curves S and $\bar{C}$ intersect earlier than normal. This corresponds to a premature awakening in the morning, another frequent sleep disorder among depressed patients.

How can sleep deprivation therapy produce an improvement? In order to explain this therapeutic effect, Anna Wirz-Justice and I had to resort to a further assumption: we presumed that the abnormally low level of process S not only affects the patients' sleep but also is causally related to the depressive symptoms. Such a relation would help to explain why depression is often most severe just after people wake up in the morning (at the low point in the curve of process S) and improves over the course of the day. Proceeding on this hypothesis, we can see that sleep deprivation would cause process S to rise to a higher level (see illustration). The increasing normalization of process S provides, in this model, the foundation for the antidepressive effect of sleep deprivation. This positive effect does

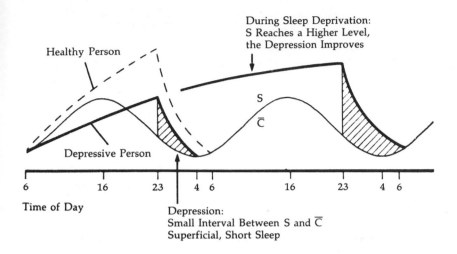

Healthy Person

During Sleep Deprivation:
S Reaches a Higher Level,
the Depression Improves

S

C̄

Depressive Person

| 6 | 16 | 23 | 4 6 | 16 | 23 | 4 6 |

Time of Day

Depression:
Small Interval Between S and C̄
Superficial, Short Sleep

FIGURE 12.3

Sleep, Sleep Deprivation, and Depression.

A hypothesis offering an explanation for the poor sleep of people suffering from depression and for the antidepressive effect of sleep deprivation. The diagram is based on the model of sleep regulation in figure 12.2. It is assumed that process S does not rise to the same levels in depressed patients as in healthy subjects. The sleep disturbances typical of depressions can be explained in terms of the smaller interval between the curves S and C̄. Sleep deprivation brings about a normalization of this interval and thus an improvement in the depression. The effect is short-lived, however, since one period of sleep is sufficient to reestablish the original conditions.

not last long, however, since the first period of sleep (coinciding with a drop to a low level in process S) usually leads to a relapse into depression.

In collaboration with David Kupfer, a psychiatrist and sleep researcher at the University of Pittsburgh, and his research group, my group in Zurich recently analyzed the sleep EEGs of depressed patients, and obtained results consistent with an impairment of process S. Other research groups are now at work testing this hypothesis. If it should emerge that their observations are incompatible with the model suggested here, other variants will have to be considered. It is nonetheless significant that the model we have developed for normal sleep regulation can be extended to account for certain pathological changes in sleep.

A Look at the Past

If research on biological processes in highly developed forms of life appears to have run into a dead end, it is often helpful to remember the evolutionary perspective. How helpful is this approach in understanding sleep regulation?

In the model described above we assume the operation of two separate processes. Process C, which regulates circadian sleep propensity, can be traced back to the simplest forms of life. We have already seen that circadian rhythms can be found throughout the plant and animal kingdoms and that they are present even in one-celled organisms (chapters 7 and 11). Circadian rest/activity rhythms, which continue to operate independently of zeitgebers in the environment, were described in insects and mollusks (chapter 7). Of course, the "sleep" of such creatures, whose nervous systems are constructed differently from those of vertebrates, cannot be defined by EEG criteria. Their circadian rest/activity rhythm might represent a precursor of the sleep/wake rhythm, however, as was suggested earlier. Both the appearance of circadian rhythms early in evolutionary history and their wide distribution indicate that adaptation to a twenty-four-hour diurnal rhythm was very important for survival. On the other hand circadian rhythms do not offer advantages only, for they are often rigidly programmed and do not adjust rapidly to changed conditions. It is thus reasonable to suppose that an additional mechanism (process S) evolved, which permitted the timing of rest and activity according to the circumstances and needs of the moment and which was not dictated by a strict schedule. This more recent process of sleep regulation must have offered the organism greatly increased flexibility and adaptability. Seen in this perspective, the development of sleep made it possible for living creatures to escape the unyielding control of their "internal clock" without having to give up all its advantages.

With these ideas in mind, let us now take another look at the sleep stages. Scientists are inclined to consider REM sleep as a "primitive" form of sleep, because it is largely determined by circadian factors. This assumption is consistent with the fact that its regulation is relatively crude. REM sleep is thus not affected by sleep deprivation for one night or by sleep during the day. It takes a massive REM sleep deficit to induce a regulatory response.

Deep sleep, by contrast, is controlled by subtle regulatory mechanisms. Although it is almost unaffected by circadian factors, it responds with great precision to changes in the preceding waking time. Sleep deprivation leads to an increase in the percentage of deep sleep; extended sleep in the morning or daytime sleep reduces deep sleep in the following night. Let us recall here that it is the slow EEG waves in non-REM sleep that determine the percentage of deep sleep. For this reason the compensatory reactions involving deep sleep need not affect the total sleep time. The slow waves can be regarded as reflecting the intensity of non-REM sleep; whereas different levels of intensity seem to exist in non-REM sleep, there is no comparable intensity aspect in REM sleep. Compensation of a REM sleep deficit can therefore occur only through the increase in REM sleep duration. This means in turn that catching up on lost REM sleep must take place at the expense of other sleep stages or even of waking time, a mechanism that may entail added risks for the organism.

The hypothesis that REM sleep represents a "primitive" form of sleep fits with our knowledge that the nerve cells that trigger it are located in the brainstem, an old and primitive part of the human brain, in evolutionary terms. The structures connected with deep sleep, on the other hand, appear to lie in the "newer" regions of the forebrain. As a final factor, REM sleep also appears much earlier in individual development than does deep sleep. Nevertheless, we must proceed with caution and not interpret the evolutionary side of this question too literally, since the sleep stages typical of mammals cannot always be identified unequivocally in the sleep of simpler kinds of animals.

The Riddle of REM Sleep

Ever since the discovery of REM sleep, scientists have been offering different explanations for this unique phenomenon. In the early days attention was focused on the presumed connection between REM sleep and dreams. But as we have seen, this link is not as close as first supposed, for it soon became clear that dreams occur outside of REM sleep. Therefore this stage cannot be equated with "dream sleep."

Another interesting hypothesis developed from the observation that this sleep stage predominates in the early years of life in human beings and animals. There are indications that mammals spend a large amount of the time before birth in a condition similar to REM sleep. Jouvet has assumed, on the basis of this finding, that REM sleep has a special role: it may serve to program processes in the brain necessary for the development and maintenance of genetically determined functions, such as instincts. According to this hypothesis, REM sleep generates a sensory activity pattern in the brain—the dream—that is independent of the external world. A motor pattern of nerve cell activity develops as well, but it is not expressed in actual behavior, because of the strong inhibition of the voluntary-muscle tone that prevails during this sleep stage. We have already described the animal experiments in which it was demonstrated that highly emotional behavior can occur during REM sleep if these inhibitions are removed. A phasic activity of nerve cells in deep brain structures occurs in REM sleep and can be measured by electrodes; this activity can be observed externally as sporadic rapid eye movements. Jouvet is inclined to think that this represents a code capable of activating information stored in genes. Such information would consist mainly of inborn, instinctive behavior, which is "practiced" during REM sleep, so to speak, and combined with acquired or learned information. Although this hypothesis is interesting, it is not easy to test in concrete experiments.

Other scientists regard REM sleep as a stage that permits specific processes of recovery or regeneration in the brain. The American sleep researcher Fred Snyder has formulated a theory known as the sentinel hypothesis. Observing that EEG patterns in REM sleep resemble waking patterns and that short periods of wakefulness frequently occur at the end of REM sleep periods, Snyder suggests that this stage has the function of allowing animals to check their surroundings periodically for signs of danger. However, this explanation is not easy to test either. An extreme position is taken by the English sleep specialist Ray Meddis, who maintains that REM sleep is an evolutionary vestige or carryover from the developmental stage of reptiles and no longer serves any purpose whatsoever in mammals. Other hypotheses were discussed in chapter 4.

These widely differing proposals illustrate how mysterious the function of REM sleep remains. The value of existing theories must be tested in further experiments, but it is just as possible that scientists will have to devise experiments of an entirely new kind to probe more deeply the mysteries of this fascinating sleep stage.

In Conclusion

Even if we are not yet in a position to give a full answer to the question of why we sleep, we possess information that may indicate useful paths to pursue. The process of sleep can be regarded as a form of adaptation to both internal and external conditions. By "imposing" a period of rest, sleep helps an organism avoid dangers in the environment, both inanimate (cold, darkness) and animate (predators). The circadian periodicity of sleep ensures that an animal does not leave its hiding place at hazardous hours. Many rodents are nocturnal creatures for this reason and spend the day—when their enemies would pose a great threat—asleep in their nests. Predators, on the other hand, have to adapt themselves to the sleep habits of their prey, in order to hunt it. In contrast to the live prey of predatory animals, the food supply of herbivores is equally available night and day, so they would derive little benefit from limiting their sleep to a particular time segment. Therefore the short sleep periods of certain gregarious animals like cows and sheep are distributed over the whole day. The American sleep researcher Wilse Webb has pointed out the advantages of this behavior to animals who live mainly in open fields or in spaces offering few hiding places. The nature of plant food forces them to eat almost without interruption, but the fact that these animals live in herds no doubt increases their safety while they sleep; some of them are awake at any given moment and thus able to react quickly if enemies approach. It is nonetheless striking that even the most threatened kinds of gregarious wild animals, such as gazelles, have to sleep at times. Obviously, animals can reduce their sleep to a minimum, but they cannot do without it. This is also true of dolphins, which must keep in constant motion in the water. As we saw, they have adapted their sleep in a unique manner, in that only half of their brain sleeps at one time.

Sleep can be regarded as a process of adaptation to conditions existing within an organism as well. An organism consumes less energy when its metabolic rate and loss of body heat are reduced. The inactivity of sleeping creatures can thus be understood as a form of economy in view of limited energy resources, which would quickly be exhausted by uninterrupted activity.

We can observe adaptations to internal and external circumstances taking place in human beings as well as in animals. The custom of the siesta, which is so common in hot countries, is a good example of how sleep/wake behavior can be adjusted to climatic conditions. But sleep certainly also serves to protect organisms from the exhaustion that would result from their remaining active too long. Just as we usually eat at regular intervals to avoid hunger, so does sleep at regular times have a similar preventive function.

If we were to ask the man on the street what the purpose of sleep is, however, he would not answer "adaptation" or "prevention" but "recuperation." Such an answer is, of course, based on our daily experience of going to bed tired in the evening and waking up the next morning refreshed and invigorated. But no matter how commonplace this occurrence may seem from a subjective point of view, it still cannot be analyzed or explained by science. W. R. Hess wrote in 1932:

> The special mechanisms which bring about repair during sleep are hidden in the tissues. They have not yet been fully explained; their existence is only deduced from their effects; yet they lie at the heart of the problem of sleep, and the resting of the sense-organs, muscles, and psychic functions are only accessory factors facilitating restoration within the tissues.[1]

Today, half a century later, we are still not much closer to the solution of this central question. We possess some data suggesting that processes of metabolic synthesis may be taking place during sleep. The high concentration of the growth hormone as sleep begins and the low concentration of the hormone cortisol, which plays a role in metabolic processes of degradation (chemical breakdown), offer support for this theory. But the crucial mechanisms underlying the process of recovery have not been discovered yet. Thus sleep research represents a rather special case in medical research: not only are we investigating a process that usually occurs in the dark, but we are also almost completely in the dark about its function. To shed a little light on this darkness is one of the main goals of sleep research.

One other factor deserves mention. Sleep research differs from other fields of medical research on more glamorous topics such as the circulatory system or cancer in that it is aimed not at preventing or treating life-threatening diseases but rather at understanding a natural, even trivial-seeming process. Sleep disorders seldom present an acute threat to human health or life, but they can greatly reduce a person's sense of well-being and affect the quality of life. The results of sleep research are not likely to produce sensational new cures, but they may bring some help and comfort to all the millions of people who lie awake night after night. In this sense sleep research can be termed a "gentle" discipline within the field of medicine.

In conclusion I would like to emphasize that sleep researchers are not concerned solely with intellectual discoveries, understanding, and control. As we conduct our experiments, we feel in touch with a fundamental process of life. In our encounters with sleep, we are faced with a process that appears utterly ordinary yet continues to elude our grasp. This experience conveys a sense of humility. Even if we go on using scientific methods to study the secrets of sleep, we must refrain from falling prey to arrogant expectations. In the words of the philosopher Martin Heidegger, "The transparency with which nature presents itself to us as a predictable interaction of forces may permit correct observations, but it is precisely such successes that may mislead us, so that in seeing what is correct we fail to see what is true."[2]

Appendix

Sleep Disorders
Information Leaflet

Many people have *occasional* sleep disorders. They take the form of

- A difficulty in falling asleep
- Restless sleep interrupted by frequent wakings
- Waking up too early in the morning

Sleeping Pills: A Temporary Solution

Too many people turn to sleeping pills without real necessity if they sleep badly. Sleeping pills should be prescribed by a *physician* if *severe* disorders occur. They are *highly effective medicines* and should not be taken casually.

Like many other forms of medication, sleeping pills have *undesirable side effects.*

Sleeping pills

- Do *not* bring about *natural* sleep (they change the normal progression of sleep stages).
- Often continue to work during the day, which may result in fatigue, "hangover," and impaired performance.
- Can become habit-forming and lead to dependency and *addiction* after long use.

The Causes and Meaning of Sleep Disorders

Many people experience *mild* and *occasional* sleep disorders, which should give them no grounds for concern.
They are frequently caused by

- Strong emotions (anger, fear, joy) or ideas and problems occupying the mind
- New surroundings (trips or vacations)
- Mild illnesses (influenza, colds, pain)

Severe sudden sleep disorders or *prolonged* mild sleep problems can have various physical or psychological causes. They should definitely be treated by a *physician.*

Good Sleep Through Good Sleep Habits

Observe the following guidelines:

- Go to bed every day at about the same time. A regular bedtime is important for good sleep.
- Get the amount of sleep you need to feel rested and re-freshed in the morning. Find out how much sleep *you per-*

sonally need. Some people can get along well on little sleep, while others need more.

- Sleep in a quiet, dark, well-ventilated room *on a mattress that is not too soft.*
- If you cannot sleep, *get up* and find something to do (reading, knitting, or other manual activity) until you are tired. Avoid sleeping during the day if your sleep at night is disturbed.

To be avoided during the evening hours are

- Excessive amounts of coffee, alcohol, nicotine
- Heavy meals
- Strenuous mental or physical activities

Remember: One sleepless night is no cause for concern!*

---

*Leaflet for patients prepared by the Laboratory for Experimental and Clinical Sleep Research, University of Zurich.

Notes

Chapter 1. A Historical View of Sleep

1. *Swann's Way,* trans. C. K. Scott Moncrieff (New York: Random House, 1934), 5.
2. F. J. Kuhlen, *Zur Geschichte der Schmerz-, Schlaf- und Betäubungsmittel in Mittelalter und früher Neuzeit* (Stuttgart: Deutscher Apotheker Verlag, 1983), 9.
3. Quoted in H. Tracol, "Why Sleepest Thou, O Lord?" *Parabola* 7 (1982):7.
4. Ibid.
5. Plato, *Apology,* in *Plato,* vol. 1 (Loeb Classical Library, 1953), 113.
6. Thomas Ken, "Morning Hymn," The Works of Thomas Ken (London: J. Wyat, 1721).
7. The following passages are based on the excellent survey by Kuhlen, *Zur Geschichte der Schmerz-, Schlaf- und Betäubungsmittel in Mittelalter und früher Neuzeit.*
8. Ibid., 25–26.
9. Ibid., 63.
10. The remarks in this section are based in large part on two recent papers by Prof. Peter R. Gleichmann of the Department of Social Sciences, University of Hannover, West Germany.
11. Gleichmann, "Schlafen und Schlafträume," *Journal für Geschichte* 2 (1980): 14–19.
12. *Oblomov,* trans. Ann Dunnigan (New York: New American Library, 1963), 22.

Chapter 3. Sleep: A Theme with Variations

1. T. Stöckmann and Georg Alfred Tienes, *Schlafe vor Mitternacht* (Stuttgart: Paracelsus Verlag, 1974), 19.

Chapter 4. Dreams

1. R. L. Woods and H. B. Greenhouse, *The New World of Dreams* (New York: Macmillan, 1974), 42.
2. Translated and quoted from Martin Kiessig, ed., *Dichter erzählen ihre Träume* (Stuttgart: Urachhaus, 1976), 330.
3. Friedrich Nietzsche, *The Gay Science,* trans. Walter Kaufmann (New York: Vintage, 1974), 212.
4. Sigmund Freud, *The Interpretation of Dreams,* vol. 4 of *The Standard Edition of the Complete Psychological Works,* trans. James Strachey (London: Hogarth Press, 1958), 26–27.

Notes

5. William Dement, *Some Must Watch While Some Must Sleep* (San Francisco: Freeman, 1974), 47.

6. Translated from Musil, *Tagebücher, Aphorismen, Essays und Reden* (Reinbek: Rowohlt, 1955), 433.

7. *The Republic* (Loeb Classical Library, 1935), 339.

8. "On Dreams," in *Parva naturalia* (Loeb Classical Library, 1957), 363.

9. Freud, *Interpretation of Dreams*, 55.

10. Translated from L. F. A. Maury, "Nouvelles observations sur les analogies des phénomènes du rêve et de l'aliénation mentale," *Annales médico-psychologiques,* 2d ser. 5 (1853):404.

11. *Interpretation of Dreams,* 25.

12. Kant, *Critique of Teleological Judgment* (pt. 2 of *Critique of Judgement*), trans. James Creed Meredith (Oxford: Clarendon Press, 1928), 29.

13. Freud, *Interpretation of Dreams,* 79.

14. Translated from Kiessig, *Dichter erzählen ihre Träume,* 325.

15. Freud, *Interpretation of Dreams,* 34 n. 1.

16. According to a papyrus in the Museum of Cairo, from Woods and Greenhouse, *New World of Dreams,* 23.

17. Freud, *Interpretation of Dreams,* 68–69.

18. Nietzsche, *The Dawn of Day,* vol. 9 of *Complete Works,* ed. Oscar Levy (Edinburgh and London, 1911), 131–32.

19. Freud, *Interpretation of Dreams,* 48.

20. David Foulkes, *A Grammar of Dreams* (New York: Basic Books, 1978), 96–97.

21. Translated from Kiessig, *Dichter erzählen ihre Träume,* 330.

22. Freud, *Five Lectures on Psycho-Analysis,* vol. 11 of *The Standard Edition of the Complete Psychological Works,* trans. James Strachey (London: Hogarth Press, 1957), 33.

23. Castaneda, *Journey to Ixtlan* (New York: Simon and Schuster, 1972), 127.

24. Translated from Kiessig, *Dichter erzählen ihre Träume,* 319.

Chapter 5.   Sleep and Sleeping Pills

1. Hurd, *Sleep, Insomnia and Hypnotics* (Detroit, 1891), 89–112.

Chapter 6.   "I Didn't Sleep a Wink All Night": Insomnia and Disorders of Sleeping and Waking

1. Shakespeare, *Macbeth,* act 2, sc. 2, line 36.

Chapter 7.   Sleep in Animals

1. Tauber, "Phylogeny of Sleep," in E. D. Weitzman, ed., *Advances in Sleep Research,* vol. 1 (Flushing, N.Y.: Spectrum Publications, 1974), 152.

Chapter 8. Sleep and the Brain

1. Translated from W. R. Hess, "Der Schlaf," *Schweizerische Medizinische Wochenschrift* 61 (1931):839.
2. Translated from W. R. Hess, "Der Schlaf," *Klinische Wochenschrift* 12 (1933): 129–34.
3. Translated from Hess, "Der Schlaf," *Schweizerische Medizinische Wochenschrift,* 839.

Chapter 9. The Search for Endogenous Sleep Substances

1. Translated from Piéron, *Le problème physiologique du sommeil* (Paris: Masson, 1913), 444.

Chapter 10. Sleep Deprivation

1. Translated from Friedrich Novalis, *Teplitzer Fragmente,* in *Das philosophisch-theoretische Werk* (Munich: Hanser, 1978), 2:411.
2. Huber-Weidmann, *Schlaf, Schlafstörungen, Schlafentzug* (Cologne: Kiepenheuer and Witsch, 1976).

Chapter 11. Sleep as a Biological Rhythm

1. Translated from *Histoire de l'Académie Royale des Sciences* (Paris, 1729), p. 35.

Chapter 12. The Purpose of Sleep

1. W. R. Hess, "The Autonomic Nervous System," *The Lancet,* Dec. 3 (1932): 1199.
2. Translated from Heidegger, *Die Frage nach der Technik: Vorträge und Aufsätze* (Pfullingen: Neske, 1967), 26.

Bibliography

The following list has been compiled for readers who wish to study specific topics of sleep research in more detail. The list includes research articles, reviews, and books.

Chapter 1. A Historical View of Sleep

For citations concerning Eastern philosophy on sleep, see H. Tracol, "Why Sleepest Thou, O Lord?" *Parabola* 7 (1982):6–9.

Chapter 2. Scientists Investigate Sleep: The Different Stages of Sleep

The first study of the human sleep EEG is A. L. Loomis, E. N. Harvey, and G. A. Hobart, "Cerebral States during Sleep, as studied by Human Brain Potentials," *Journal of Experimental Psychology* 21 (1937):127–44.

For the classic book on sleep research, see N. Kleitman, *Sleep and Wakefulness*, 2nd Edition (Chicago: The University of Chicago Press, 1963).

The first descriptions of REM sleep in man are in: E. Aserinsky and N. Kleitman, "Regularly Occurring Periods of Eye Motility and Concomitant Phenomena during Sleep," *Science* 118 (1953):273–74; and W. C. Dement and N. Kleitman, "Cyclic Variations in EEG During Sleep and Their Relation to Eye Movements, Body Motility, and Dreaming," *Electroencephalography and Clinical Neurophysiology* 9 (1957):673–90.

For a discussion of the generally adopted sleep stage criteria, see *A Manual of Standardized Terminology, Techniques, and Scoring System for Sleep Stages of Human Subjects*, National Institutes of Health Publication 204, ed. A. Rechtschaffen and A. Kales (Washington, D.C.: US Government Printing Office, 1968).

For a discussion of the non–REM/REM cycle see: H. Schulz, et al., "The REM-NREM Sleep Cycle: Renewal Process or Periodically Driven Process?" *Sleep* 2 (1980):319–28.

For an all-night spectral analysis of the sleep EEG, see A. A. Borbély et al., "Sleep-deprivation: Effect on Sleep Stages and EEG Power Density in Man," *Electroencephalography and Clinical Neurophysiology* 51 (1981):483–93.

Hormones and sleep are examined in T. Åkerstedt, "Hormones and Sleep," in A. A. Borbély and J. L. Valatx, eds., *Sleep Mechanisms Experimental Brain Research*, vol. 8, suppl. (Heidelberg, W. Germany: Springer-Verlag, 1984), 193–203.

For a discussion of the phallogram in sleep, see I. Karacan et al., "The Ontogeny of Nocturnal Penile Tumescence," *Waking and Sleeping* I (1976): 27–44.

213

Chapter 3.   Sleep: A Theme with Variations

Sleep and the sleep EEG in children are the topics of P. A. Coble, et al., "EEG Sleep of Normal Healthy Children. Part I: Findings Using Standard Measurement Methods," *Sleep* 7 (1984):289–303; and T. F. Anders and M. Keener, "Developmental Course of Nighttime Sleep-wake Patterns in Full-term and Premature Infants During the First Year of Life: I," *Sleep* 8 (1985):173–92.

For a discussion of sleep stage distribution as a function of age, see H. P. Roffwarg, J. N. Muzio, and W. C. Dement, "Ontogenetic Development of the Human Sleep-dream Cycle," *Science* 152 (1966):604–19.

The siesta habit in Greece is described in C. R. Soldatos, M. G. Madianos, and I. G. Vlachonikolis, "Early Afternoon Napping: A Fading Greek Habit," in W. P. Koella, ed., *Sleep 1982* (Basel, Switz.: Karger, 1983), 202–5.

The following publications discuss sleep in the elderly: I. Strauch and M. E. Wollschläger, "Sleep Behavior in the Aged," in U. J. Jovanovic, *The Nature of Sleep* (Stuttgart, West Germany: Gustav Fischer Verlag, 1973), 129–31; L. E. Miles and W. C. Dement, eds., "Sleep and Aging," *Sleep* 3 (1980):119–20; and R. Spiegel, *Sleep and Sleeplessness in Advanced Age* (Lancaster, Eng.: MTP Press, 1981).

Morning and evening persons are described in J. Foret et al., "Sleep and Body Temperature in 'Morning' and 'Evening' People," *Sleep* 8 (1985):311–18.

Extreme cases of short sleep are examined in: H. S. Jones and I. Oswald, "Two Cases of Healthy Insomnia," *Electroencephalography and Clinical Neurophysiology* 24 (1968):378–80; R. Meddis, A. J. D. Pearson, and G. Lanford, "An Extreme Case of Healthy Insomnia," *Electroencephalography and Clinical Neurophysiology* 35 (1973):-213–14; and I. Oswald and K. Adam, "The Man Who Had Not Slept for Ten Years," *British Medical Journal* 281 (1980):1684–85.

For an epidemiological study of sleep duration and mortality, see D. F. Kripke et al., "Short and Long Sleep and Sleeping Pills: Is Increased Mortality Associated?," *Archives of General Psychiatry* 36 (1979):103–16.

Hereditary factors and sleep duration are discussed in M. Partinen et al., "Genetic and Environmental Determination of Human Sleep," *Sleep* 6 (1983):-179–85.

Sleep stages in long and short sleepers are the topic of O. Benoit, J. Foret, and G. Bouard, "The Time Course of Slow-Wave Sleep and REM Sleep in Habitual Long and Short Sleepers: Effect of Prior Wakefulness," *Human Neurobiology* 2 (1983):91–96.

Chapter 4.   Dreams

Some general books on dreams include: R. L. Woods and W. B. Greenhouse, *The New World of Dreams* (New York: Macmillan, 1974); W. C. Dement, *Some Must Watch While Some Must Sleep* (San Francisco: W. H. Freeman, 1974); R. D. Cartwright, *Night Life Explorations in Dreaming* (Englewood, N.J.: Prentice-Hall, 1977); A. M. Arkin, J. S. Antrobus, and S. J. Ellman, *The Mind in Sleep: Psychology and Psychophysiology* (New York: John Wiley & Sons, 1978); B. B. Wolman, ed., *Handbook of Dreams: Research Theories and Applications* (New York: Van Nostrand Reinhold, 1979).

The following contains a survey of older scientific literature on the generation of dreams: *The Interpretation of Dreams*, vol. 4 of *The Standard Edition of The Complete*

Bibliography

Psychological Works of Sigmund Freud, ed. and trans. J. Strachey (London: Hogarth Press, 1953).

For an analysis of dream content, see C. Hall and R. L. Van de Castle, *The Content Analysis of Dreams* (E. Norwalk, Ct.: Appleton-Century-Crofts, 1966).

Dreams in children are discussed in: D. Foulkes, "Children's Dreams," in *Handbook of Dreams,* ed. B. B. Wolman (New York: Van Nostrand Reinhold, 1979), 131–67; D. Foulkes, "Dream Ontogeny and Dream Psychophysiology," in *Sleep Disorders: Basic and Clinical Research* (Lancaster, Eng.: MTP Press, 1983), 347–62.

For a study of dream duration, see W. Dement and E. Wolpert, "The Relation of Eye Movements, Body Motility, and External Stimuli to Dream Content," *Journal of Experimental Psychology* 55 (1958):543–53.

For a structural analysis of dreams, see D. Foulkes, *A Grammar of Dreams* (New York: Basic Books, 1978).

Neurobiological theories of dream generation are discussed in: J. A. Hobson and R. W. McCarley, "The Brain as a Dream State Generator: An Activation-Synthesis Hypothesis of the Dream Process," *American Journal of Psychiatry* 134 (1977):1335–48; M. Jouvet, "Le sommeil paradoxal est-il responsable d'une programmation génétique de cerveau?" *Comptes rendus des séances de la Société de Biologie* 172 (1978):9–30; M. Koukkou and D. Lehmann, "Psychophysiologie des Träumens und der Neurosentherapie: Das Zustands-Wechsel-Modell, eine Synopsis," *Fortschritte der Neurologie, Psychiatrie und ihrer Grenzgebiete* 48 (1980):- 324–50; and F. Crick and G. Mitchison, "The Function of Dream Sleep," *Nature* 304 (1983):111–14.

The first study of selective REM sleep deprivation is W. C. Dement, "The Effect of Dream Deprivation," *Science* 131 (1960):1705–7.

Lucid dreams are the subject of C. T. Tart, "From Spontaneous Event to Lucidity: A Review of Attempts to Consciously Control Nocturnal Dreaming," in *Handbook of Dreams,* ed. B. B. Wolman (New York: Van Nostrand Reinhold, 1979), 226–68.

Chapter 5.   Sleep and Sleeping Pills

An excellent book on hypnotics is W. B. Mendelson, *The Use and Misuse of Sleeping Pills* (New York: Plenum, 1980).

Recommendations of the Consensus Conference are outlined in "Consensus Conference, Drugs and Insomnia," *Journal of the American Medical Association* 251 (1984):2410–14.

Pharmacological properties of benzodiazepine hypnotics are discussed in D. D. Breimer and R. Jochemsen, "Pharmacokinetics of Hypnotic Drugs," in *Psychopharmacology of Sleep,* ed. D. Wheatley (New York: Raven Press, 1981):135–52.

The effects and aftereffects of hypnotics are examined in: P. Mattmann et al., "Day-time Residual Effects and Motor Activity After Three Benzodiazepine Hypnotics," *Arzneimittel-Forschung* 32 (1982):461–65; A. A. Borbély et al., "Midazolam and Triazolam: Hypnotic Action and Residual Effects After a Single Bedtime Dose," *Arzneimittel-Forschung* 33 (1983):1500–1502; and A. A. Borbély et al., "Effect of Midazolam and Sleep Deprivation on Day-time Sleep Propensity," *Arzneimittel-Forschung* 35 (1985):1696–99.

A method for monitoring ambulatory motor activity in man is presented in A. A. Borbély et al., "Langzeitregistrierung der Bewegungsaktivität: Anwendungen in Forschung und Klinik," *Schweizerische Medizinische Wochenschrift* 111 (1981):730–35.

The first study on the effect of hypnotics on sleep is I. Oswald and R. G. Priest, "Five Weeks to Escape the Sleeping-pill Habit," *British Medical Journal* 2 (1965):1093–99.

For discussions of the effect of hypnotics on sleep EEG, see: A. A. Borbély et al., "A Single Dose of Benzodiazepine Hypnotics Alters the Sleep EEG in the Subsequent Drug-free Night," *European Journal of Pharmacology* 89 (1983):157–61; and A. A. Borbély et al., "Effect of Benzodiazepine Hypnotics on All-night Sleep EEG Spectra," *Human Neurobiology* 4 (1985):189–94.

The mechanism of action of benzodiazepines is described in W. Haefely, "Tranquilizers," in *Preclinical Psychopharmacology,* ed. D. G. Grahame-Smith and P. J. Cowen (Amsterdam: Excerpta Medica, 1983), 107–51.

The effects of valerian are discussed in: P. D. Leathwood et al., "Aqueous Extract of Valerian Root (Valeriana officinalis L.) Improves Sleep Quality in Man," *Pharmacology, Biochemistry and Behaviour* 17 (1982):65–71; and G. Balderer and A. A. Borbély, "Effect of Valerian on Human Sleep," *Psychopharmacology* 87 (1985):406–9.

Chapter 6.   "I Didn't Sleep a Wink All Night": Insomnia and Disorders of Sleeping and Waking

The following are surveys of sleep quality and sleep disorders: A. A. Borbély, "Schlafgewohnheiten, Schlafqualität und Schlafmittelkonsum der Schweizer Bevölkerung," *Schweizer Aerztezeitung* 65 (1984):1606–13; G. D. Mellinger, M. B. Balter, and E. H. Uhlenluth, "Insomnia and Its Treatment," *Archives of General Psychiatry* 42 (1985):225–32.

For a classification of sleep and wake disorders, see Association of Sleep Disorders Centers, "Diagnostic Classification of Sleep and Arousal Disorders," 1st ed., *Sleep* 2 (1979):1–137.

Non-drug treatments of sleep disorders are discussed in W. B. Mendelson, "Nonpharmacologic Treatment of Insomnia." In *The Use and Misuse of Sleeping Pills* (New York: Plenum, 1980), 163–75.

For surveys of sleep disorders see: J. M. Gaillard, "Physiologie du sommeil et physiopathologie de l'insomnie," *Schweizerische Medizinische Wochenschrift* 109 (1979):97–103; and P. Hauri, *The Sleep Disorders: Current Concepts* (Kalamazoo, Mich.: The Upjohn Company, 1982).

Somnambulism is the topic of A. Jacobson et al., "Somnambulism: All-night Electroencephalographic Studies," *Science* 148 (1965):975–77.

Snoring and sleep apnea are examined in E. Garfield, "Sleep Disorders," *Current Contents* 22 (1983):5–10; 23 (1983):5–11.

Chapter 7.   Sleep in Animals

For a discussion of natural sleep behavior, see H. Hediger, "Natural Sleep Behavior in Vertebrates." In *Functions of the Nervous System,* ed. M. Monnier and M. Meulders (Amsterdam: Elsevier, 1983), 105–30.

Bibliography

The sleep EEG in the rat is discussed in relation to normative studies and the effect of sleep deprivation in: A. A. Borbély and H. U. Neuhaus, "Sleep-deprivation: Effects on Sleep and EEG in the Rat," *Journal of Comparative Physiology* 133 (1979):71–87; and A. A. Borbély, I. Tobler, and M. Hanagasioglu, "Effect of Sleep Deprivation on Sleep and EEG Power Spectra in the Rat," *Behavioral Brain Research* 14 (1984):171–82.

For a survey of sleep in different animal species, see H. Zepelin and A. Rechtschaffen, "Mammalian Sleep, Longevity and Energy Metabolism," *Brain Behavior and Evolution* 10 (1974):425–70.

For discussions of the evolution of sleep see: E. S. Tauber, "Phylogeny of Sleep," in *Advances in Sleep Research,* ed. E. D. Weitzman, vol. 1 (Flushing, N.Y.: Spectrum Publications, 1974), 133–72; I. Tobler and J. Horne, eds., "Phylogenetic Approaches to the Functions of Sleep," *Sleep 1982,* ed. W. P. Koella (Basel, Switz.: Karger, 1983), 126–46; I. Tobler, "Evolution of the Sleep Process: A Phylogenetic Approach," *Sleep Mechanisms: Experimental Brain Research,* ed. A. A. Borbély and J. L. Valatx, vol. 8, suppl. (Heidelberg, W. Germany: Springer-Verlag, 1984), 227–38; and S. S. Campbell and I. Tobler, "Animal Sleep: A Review of Sleep Duration Across Phylogeny," *Neuroscience and Biobehavioral Reviews* 8 (1984):269–300.

Sleep in the dolphin is described in L. M. Mukhametov, "Sleep in Marine Mammals." In *Sleep Mechanisms. Experimental Brain Research,* ed. A. A. Borbély and J. L. Valatx, vol. 8, suppl. (Heidelberg, W. Germany: Springer-Verlag, 1984), 227–38.

For an examination of sleep in insects, see I. Tobler, "Effect of Forced Locomotion on the Rest-Activity Cycle of the Cockroach," *Behavioral Brain Research* 8 (1983):351–60.

Rest and rest deprivation in fish is discussed in I. Tobler and A. A. Borbély, "Effect of Rest Deprivation on Motor Activity in Fish," *Journal of Comparative Physiology* 157 (1985):817–22.

Circadian rhythms in plants are described in E. Bünning, *The Physiological Clock* (Heidelberg, W. Germany: Springer-Verlag, 1973).

For a discussion of sleep regulation in animals, see A. A. Borbély, "Sleep Regulation: Circadian Rhythm and Homeostasis." In *Sleep. Clinical and Experimental Aspects. Current Topics in Neuroendocrinology,* vol. 1, ed. D. Ganten and D. Pfaff (Heidelberg, W. Germany: Springer-Verlag, 1982), 83–103.

Hibernation and torpor are topics of J. M. Walker and R. J. Berger, "Sleep as an Adaptation for Energy Conservation Functionally Related to Hibernation and Shallow Torpor," *Progress in Brain Research* 53 (1980):255–78; T. S. Kilduff et al., "[14c] 2-Deoxyglucose Uptake in Ground-Squirrel Brain during Hibernation," *The Journal of Neuroscience* 2 (1982):143–57.

Chapter 8.   Sleep and the Brain

For a historical survey of the neurophysiology of sleep, see G. Moruzzi, "The Sleep-Waking Cycle," *Ergebnisse der Physiologie* 64 (1972):1–165.

The monoamine theory of sleep regulation is discussed in: M. Jouvet, "The Role of Monoamines and Acetylcholine-containing Neurons in the Regulation of the Sleep-waking Cycle," *Ergebnisse der Physiologie* 64 (1972):166–307; and M. Jouvet, "Neuropharmacology of the Sleep-waking Cycle," in *Handbook of Psycho-*

pharmacology, vol. 8, ed. S. D. Iversen, L. L. Iversen, and S. H. Snyder (New York: Plenum, 1977), 233–93.

Contradictory findings with respect to the monoamine theory are presented in A. A. Borbély, "Pharmacological Approaches to Sleep Regulation," in *Sleep Mechanisms and Functions in Humans and Animals—An Evolutionary Perspective*, ed. A. Mayes (New York: Van Nostrand Reinhold, 1983), 232–61.

For discussions of REM sleep mechanisms in the brain stem see: A. R. Morrison, "A Window on the Sleeping Brain," *Scientific American*, April 1983, 86–94; E. Vivaldi, R. W. McCarley, and J. A. Hobson, "Evocation of Desynchronized Sleep Signs by Chemical Microstimulation of the Pontine Brain Stem," in *The Reticular Formation Revisited*, ed. J. A. Hobson and M.A.B. Brazier (New York: Raven Press, 1980), 513–59; and J. C. Gillin, N. Sitaram, and W. B. Mendelson, "Acetylcholine, Sleep and Depression," *Human Neurobiology* 1 (1982):211–19.

New sleep research methods are described in R. Cespuglio et al., "Voltametric Detection of Brain 5-Hydroxyindolamines: A New Technology Applied to Sleep Research," in *Sleep Mechanisms: Experimental Brain Research*, vol. 8, suppl., ed. A. A. Borbély and J. L. Valatx (Heidelberg, W. Germany: Springer-Verlag, 1984), 95–105.

Chapter 9.   The Search for Endogenous Sleep Substances

Piéron discusses his "classic" experiments and theories in H. Piéron, *Le problème physiologique du sommeil* (Paris: Masson, 1913).

Recent reviews and books include: A. A. Borbély and I. Tobler, "The Search for an Endogenous 'Sleep Substance,' " *Trends in Pharmacological Sciences* 1 (1980):-356–58; S. Inoué, K. Uchizono, and H. Nagasaki, "Endogenous Sleep-promoting Factors," *Trends in Neurosciences* 5 (1982):218–20; R. Ursin and A. A. Borbély, eds., "Endogenous Sleep Factors," in *Sleep 1982*, ed. W. P. Koella (Basel, Switz.: Karger, 1983), 106–25; M. Jouvet, "Indoleamines and Sleep-inducing Factors," in *Sleep Mechanisms: Experimental Brain Research*, vol. 8, suppl., ed. A. A. Borbély and J. L. Valatx (Heidelberg, W. Germany: Springer-Verlag, 1984), 118–32; J. M. Krueger, "Somnogenic Activity of Muramyl Peptides," *Trends in Pharmacological Sciences* 6 (1985):218–221; and S. Inoué and A. A. Borbély, eds., *Endogenous Sleep Substances and Sleep Regulation* (Utrecht, Neth.: VNU Science Press, 1985).

Recent research papers on endogenous substances include: R. Ueno et al., "Prostaglandin D2, A Cerebral Sleep-inducing Substance in Rats," *Proceedings of the National Academy of Science, USA*, 80 (1983):1735–37; and J. M. Krueger et al., "Sleep-promoting Effects of Endogenous Pyrogen (Interleukin-1)," *American Journal of Physiology* 246 (1984):R994–99.

Chapter 10.   Sleep Deprivation

J. A. Horne, "A Review of the Biological Effects of Total Sleep Deprivation in Man," *Biological Psychology* 7 (1978):55–102.

One of the first studies of sleep deprivation is G. T. W. Patrick and J. A.

Gilbert, "On the Effects of Loss of Sleep," *The Psychological Review* 3 (1896):- 469–83.

The world record sleep-deprivation case is described in G. Gulevich, W. Dement, and L. Johnson, "Psychiatric and EEG Observations on a Case of Prolonged (264-hour) Wakefulness," *Archives of General Psychiatry* 15 (1966):- 29–35.

For a discussion of performance tests during sleep deprivation, see H. L. Williams et al., "Impaired Performance with Acute Sleep Loss," *Psychological Monographs* 73 (1959):1–26.

The gradual shortening of sleep duration is examined in D. J. Mullaney et al., "Sleep During and After Gradual Sleep Reduction," *Psychophysiology* 14 (1977):- 237–44.

Chronic sleep reduction is the subject of W. B. Webb and H. W. Agnew, Jr., "Are We Chronically Sleep Deprived?" *Bulletin of the Psychonomic Society* 6 (1975):- 47–8.

For a discussion of daytime sleepiness, see M. Carskadon, ed., "Current Perspectives on Daytime Sleepiness," *Sleep* 5, suppl. 2 (1982):55–202.

Articles concerning the effects of sleep deprivation in animals include A. A. Borbély and H. U. Neuhaus, "Sleep-deprivation: Effects on Sleep and EEG in the Rat," *Journal of Comparative Physiology*, 133 (1979):71–87; and I. Tobler, "Deprivation of Sleep and Rest in Vertebrates and Invertebrates," in *Endogenous Sleep Substances and Sleep Regulation,* ed. S. Inoué and A. A. Borbély (Utrecht, Neth.: VNU Science Press, 1985), 57–66.

For discussions of sleep deprivation and depression, see R. H. Van den Hoofdakker and D.G.M. Beersma, "Sleep Deprivation, Mood, and Sleep Physiology," in *Sleep Mechanisms. Experimental Brain Research,* vol. 8, suppl., ed. A. A. Borbély and J. L. Valatx (Heidelberg, W. Germany: Springer-Verlag, 1984), 297–309; and J. C. Gillin and A. A. Borbély, "Sleep: A Neurobiological Window on Affective Disorders," *Trends in Neurosciences* 8 (1985):537–42.

Chapter 11.   Sleep as a Biological Rhythm

Long-term ambulatory activity monitoring in man is described in A. A. Borbély, "Long-term Recording of Rest-activity Cycle in Man." In *Application of Behavioral Pharmacology in Toxicology,* ed. G. Zbinden et al. (New York: Raven Press, 1983), 39–44.

Books and articles on sleep in man under "time-free" conditions include: M. Siffre, *Expériences hors du temps* (Paris: Fayard, 1972); R. A. Wever, *The Circadian System of Man* (Heidelberg, W. Germany: Springer-Verlag, 1979); J. Zulley, *Der Einfluss von Zeitgebern auf den Schlaf des Menschen* (Frankfurt: Fischer, 1979); C. A. Czeisler et al., "Human Sleep: Its Duration and Organization Depend on Its Circadian Phase," *Science* 210 (1980):1264–67; and E. Weitzman, "Chronobiology of Man: Sleep, Temperature and Neuroendocrine Systems," *Human Neurobiology* 1 (1982):173–83.

The classic paper on the site of the internal clock is F. Stephan and I. Zucker, "Circadian Rhythms in Drinking Behavior and Locomotor Activity of Rats are Eliminated by Hypothalamic Lesions," *Proceedings of the National Academy of Science, USA* 69 (1972):1583–86.

Two recent books on the subject are J. Aschoff, S. Daan, and G. A. Groos, *Vertebrate Circadian Systems: Structure and Physiology* (Heidelberg, W. Germany: Springer-Verlag, 1982); and M. C. Moore-Ede, F. M. Sulzman, and C. A. Fuller, *The Clocks That Time Us: Physiology of the Circadian Timing System* (Cambridge, Mass.: Harvard University Press, 1982).

For a discussion of sleep regulation after elimination of the "internal clock," see I. Tobler, A. A. Borbély, and G. Groos, "The Effect of Sleep Deprivation on Sleep in Rats with Suprachiasmatic Lesions," *Neuroscience Letters* 42 (1983):49–54.

Sleep and circadian rhythms are examined in G. Groos, "The Physiological Organization of the Circadian Sleep-wake Cycle," in *Sleep Mechanisms. Experimental Brain Research*, vol. 8, suppl., ed. A. A. Borbély and J. L. Valatx (Heidelberg, W. Germany: Springer-Verlag, 1984), 241–57.

The experiment with biased watches is described in P. R. Lewis and M. C. Lobban, "Dissociation of Diurnal Rhythms in Human Subjects Living in Abnormal Time Routines," *Quarterly Journal of Experimental Physiology* 42 (1957):-371–86.

The question of whether there are one or two circadian oscillators is addressed in R. E. Kronauer et al., "Mathematical Model of the Human Circadian System with Two Interacting Oscillators," *American Journal of Physiology* 242 (1982):3–17; and S. Daan, D.G.M. Beersma, and A. A. Borbély, "The Timing of Human Sleep: Recovery Process Gated by a Circadian Pacemaker," *American Journal of Physiology* 246 (1984):R161–78.

For a discussion of shift-work, sleep, and circadian rhythms see T. Åkerstedt and M. Gillberg, "Displacement of the Sleep Period and Sleep Deprivation," *Human Neurobiology* 1 (1982):163–71; and C. A. Czeisler, M. C. Moore-Ede, and R. M. Coleman, "Rotating Shift Work Schedules that Disrupt Sleep Are Improved by Applying Circadian Principles," *Science* 217 (1982):101–13.

Shifting rhythms as a therapeutic measure is discussed in T. A. Wehr et al., "Phase Advance of the Circadian Sleep-Wake Cycle as an Antidepressant," *Science* 206 (1979):710–13; and C. A. Czeisler et al., "Chrono-therapy: Resetting the Circadian Clocks of Patients with Delayed Sleep-Phase Insomnia," *Sleep* 4 (1981):1–21.

Chapter 12.   The Purpose of Sleep

For a study of sleep and locomotor activity in the animal, see M. Hanagasioglu and A. A. Borbély, "Effect of Voluntary Locomotor Activity on Sleep in the Rat," *Behavioral Brain Research* 4 (1982):359–68.

The circadian rhythm of sleepiness during sleep deprivation is examined in T. Åkerstedt and J. E. Fröberg, "Psychophysiological Circadian Rhythms in Women During 72 Hours of Sleep Deprivation," *Waking and Sleeping* I (1977):-387–94.

The two-process model of sleep regulation is described in A. A. Borbély, "A Two-Process Model of Sleep Regulation," *Human Neurobiology* I (1982):195–204; and S. Daan and D. Beersma, "Circadian Gating of Human Sleep and Wakefulness," in *Mathematical Models of the Circadian Sleep-Wake Cycle*, ed. M. C. Moore-Ede and C. A. Czeisler (New York: Raven Press, 1983), 129–58.

For discussions of sleep regulation and depression, see A. A. Borbély and A. Wirz-Justice, "Sleep, Sleep Deprivation and Depression: A Hypothesis Derived from a Model of Sleep Regulation," *Human Neurobiology* 1 (1982):205–10; and J. C. Gillin and A. A. Borbély, "Sleep: A Neurobiological Window on Affective Disorders," *Trends in Neurosciences* 8 (1985):537–42.

The mystery of REM sleep is examined in R. Meddis, *The Sleep Instinct* (London: Routledge and Kegan Paul, 1977); M. Jouvet, "Does a Genetic Programming of the Brain Occur During Paradoxical Sleep?" in *Cerebral Correlates of Conscious Experience,* ed. P. Buser and A. Rougeul-Buser (Amsterdam: Elsevier, 1978), 245–61; and F. Snyder, "Toward an Evolutionary Theory of Dreaming," *American Journal of Psychiatry* 123 (1966):121–42.

For a discussion of theories of sleep, see W. B. Webb, "Theories in Modern Sleep Research." In *Sleep Mechanisms and Functions in Humans and Animals—An Evolutionary Perspective,* ed. A. Mayes (New York: Van Nostrand Reinhold, 1983), 1–17.

Index

Ackermann, J. F., 12
Adam, 6, 10, 11
Adrian, E. D., 18
Agnew, H., 160
Akerstedt, T., 193
Alcohol, 70, 73, 84, 85, 94
Alexander of Aphrodisias, 10
Animals, 105–21; amphibians, 115; apes, 106; aplysia, 115; bat, 108–9, 120; bear, 105, 108, 121; bird, 106, 112, 114–15; cat, 106, 110–11, 131; chameleon, 114; cockroach, 119; corporate vigilance in, 114; cow, 110–11, 204; dolphin, 108, 111–12, 204; dormouse, 120; dozing in, 111; echidna, 108; elephant, 106, 110–11; "family tree" of, 112–13; fish, 115; fly, 117; fox, 106; frog, 115; gazella, 204; groundhog, 105, 120; guinea pig, 110; hamster, 105, 120; hibernation in, 105, 120; horse, 106, 110–11; hyena, 106; invertebrates, 115; kangaroo, 106; lethargy in, 121; lion, 108; mammals, 106, 109; migration of, 114; mole, 110; mollusk, 115; monotreme, 108; moth, 115–16; mouse, 110; nonREM/REM sleep cycle in, 109–10; opposum, 110; parrot fish, 115; pig, 111; pigeon, 114; place for sleeping of, 106; polyphasic sleep in, 109; porcupine, 110, 120; prairie dog, 121; predator, 204; rabbit, 106, 108–9, 140; rat, 106, 108–11, 117–19, 163, 179, 192; reptiles, 114–15; rest-activity rhythm in, 99, 116–17, 119–20; rest deprivation in, 120; rodents, 106, 204; seal, 106; sheep, 111, 204; sleep behavior in, 115; sleep deprivation in, 118, 120, 149, 151, 192; sleep duration in, 109; sleep nest of, 106; sleep position of, 107; sleep ritual of, 106; sleep tree of, 106; sleep in the young of, 110; slug, 115; spiny anteater, 108; squirrel, 121; torpor in, 115, 121; unihemispheric sleep in, 111; weasel, 120
Arendt, J., 146
Aristotle, 10, 58, 105
Artemidorus, 63, 64
Aschoff, J., 117, 173, 179
Aserinsky, E., 22
Athena, 63

Baeyer, A. von, 71
Balderer, G., 84
Barbiturates, 71
Bedroom, 13–14
Beersma, D., 183, 197
Belladonna, 71
Benoit, O., 44
Benz, E., 152
Benzodiazepine receptor, 83
Benzodiazepines, 73, 77, 86
Berger, H., 17–18
Biological rhythms, 104, 116, 170–190; and bunker experiments, 173, 175; circadian oscillators in, 185; circadian rhythm in, 179; delayed sleep phase syndrome in, 189; in depression, 189; desynchronization in, 184–85; disturbance of, 186; of fatigue, 194; free-running, 184; of hormones, 187; jetlag and, 186; and light/dark cycle, 181; and phase-shift therapy, 188; shift work and, 187–88; suprachiasmatic nuclei and, 182–83; in a "time-free" environment, 172
Boerhaave, H., 11
Bonnet, M., 39
Brain mechanism, 122–135; and acetylcholine, 130, 132; and cortisol, 205; and endogenous sleep substances, 197; and endorphins, 137; and enkephalins, 137; and factor S,

Index

Rapid Eye Movement sleep, *see* REM sleep
Rechtschaffen, A., 26, 29, 49
REM sleep, 22, 35–36, 48, 53, 78, 92, 100, 108, 110, 114, 118, 127, 130–31, 163, 176, 197, 201–2
REM sleep deprivation, 79
REM sleep rebound, 166
REM sleep substance, 144
Rest-activity rhythm, 99, 116–17, 119–20, 170–71
Rest deprivation, 120
Reticular formation, 125
Richter, K., 181
Riou, F., 146
Robert, W., 62
Romeo, 7, 38
Ruckebusch, Y., 111

Sachs, J., 142
Saint-Paul, U., 117
Sandman, 6
Schnedorf, J. G., 139
Schoenenberger, G., 143–44
Senoi, 68
Sentinel hypothesis of REM sleep, 203
Shakespeare, W., 7, 38, 70
Shift work, 104, 187–88
Short sleepers, 40
Siesta, 35, 205
Siffre, M., 173–74
Sitaram, N., 132
Slack, 5
Sleep: "active" sleep, 33; at different ages, 31; animal spirits and, 11; blood pressure during, 30; body functions during, 29; body movements in, 24, 77; body temperature during, 30; breathing during, 30, 33; in childhood, 35; during daytime, 14; death and, 5–7; deep sleep, 8, 23, 201; delta sleep, 23, 118; depth of, 17, 20, 163; disorders of, 207; duration of, 11, 42, 45; in the elderly, 36; erections during, 30; etymology of word, 4–6; evolution of, 112, 116, 200; history of, 3–15, 27; hormonal changes during, 30; hygiene, 94,

208; intensity of, 118, 162; laboratory, 18; metabolic rate during, 205; before midnight, 38; and mortality rate, 45–46; origin of, 112; oxygen and, 12; paralysis, 100; from philosophy to science, 10; places and times for, 13; polyphasic pattern of, 31; profile, 22, 27, 79, 85; pulse during, 30, 33; purpose of, 191–206; "quiet," 33; and recuperation, 205; regulation of, 118; restorative powers of, 40; ritual of, 106; sociology of, 13; stages of, 16, 20, 22–25; "staircase" of, 25; state of blessedness, 8; state of dull ignorance, 8; states of, 8; substances of, *see* Endogenous sleep substance; in twins, 44; waking up from, 3; walking during, 96–97
Sleep deprivation, 151–169, 198, 201; in brainwashing, 152; chronic, 160; and daytime sleep propensity, 159; and deep sleep, 163, 201; and depression, 168, 198; EEG spectral analysis of, 163; effect on performance of, 151, 157–58; effect on sleep stages of, 162; experimental, 153, 155; fatigue during, 193; hallucinations during, 156; and micro sleep, 156, 158; and Multiple Sleep Latency Test, 160–61; during pannichides, 152; partial, 158; and psychosis, 156; recovery sleep after, 162; of REM sleep, 163, 165–66; selective, 165; stage 4, rebound after, 167; therapy, 168; in *tortura insomniae*, 152; in *tortura vigiliae*, 152; world record of, 154
Sleep disorders, 207
Sleeping Beauty, 7
Sleeping pills, 36, 47, 70–86, 88, 96, 207–8; addiction to, 72–73; aftereffects of, 81; barbiturates, 71; benzodiazepines, 73, 77, 86; chloralhydrate, 71; consumption of, 70; EEG spectral analysis and, 79; effectiveness of, 74; effects in the elderly of, 82; effects on sleep of, 78; elimination half-life of, 73; herbal preparations, 85; mechanism of action of, 82; and "natural medi-